Floral Doilies for Crocheting

Edited by
RITA WEISS

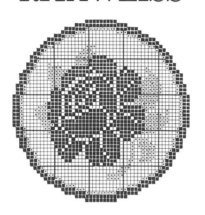

Dover Publications, Inc.
New York

American terminology, which is different from crochet terminology in most other parts of the world, is used for the stitches in this book. The following chart supplies the American name of crochet stitches and their equivalent in other countries. Crocheters should become thoroughly familiar with the differences in these terms before starting on any project.

AMERICAN NAME	EQUIVALENT
Chain	same
Slip	Single crochet
Single crochet	Double crochet
Half-double or short-double crochet	Half-treble crochet
Double crochet	Treble crochet
Treble crochet	Double-treble crochet
Double-treble crochet	Treble-treble crochet
Treble-treble or long-treble crochet	Quadruple-treble crochet
Afghan stitch	Tricot crochet

Published in Canada by General Publishing Company, Ltd., 30 Lesmill Road, Don Mills, Toronto, Ontario.
Published in the United Kingdom by Constable and Company, Ltd., 10 Orange Street, London WC2H 7EG.

This Dover edition, first published in 1979, is a new selection of patterns from *Flower Doilies and a New Pansy Doily*, published by the American Thread Company in 1949; *Doilies* by Carolyn Graeves, published by the Spool Cotton Company in 1942; *Hand Crochet by Royal Society*, published by Royal Society, Inc., in 1945; *Floral Doilies, Book No. 258*, published by the Spool Cotton Company in 1949; *Chair Sets and Runners, Book No. 261*, published by the Spool Cotton Company in 1949 and *Doilies, Luncheon Sets, Table Runners, Book No. 147*, published by the Spool Cotton Company in 1940. A new introduction has been especially written for this edition.

International Standard Book Number: 0-486-23789-3
Library of Congress Catalog Card Number: 78-74122

Manufactured in the United States of America
Dover Publications, Inc.
180 Varick Street
New York, N.Y. 10014

INTRODUCTION

The crocheting of beautiful lace doilies is becoming one of the most popular crafts today, and the floral doily pattern is high on the list of everyone's favorites. This is a new collection of some of the most beautiful floral doily patterns published in instruction brochures over thirty years ago when hand-made lace was an important part of every home.

Today as more crocheters rediscover that elusive, intrinsic joy that comes with creating a handmade article, the locating of crochet patterns has become the most difficult part of making a beautiful heirloom. This book and others in this series (*Crocheting Doilies*, 0-486-23424-X; *Crocheting Bedspreads*, 0-486-23610-2 and *Crocheting Placemats*, 0-486-23700-1) are intended to fill that need. There are patterns here for the master crocheter who can use them as a springboard for her own creative endeavors, for the novice in the art of the crochet hook who can learn her first lessons while making a beautiful floral doily, and for those who feel a bit of crocheted lace is a creative expression that transcends mere functionalism.

Although many of the threads listed with the patterns are still available, you may wish to substitute some of the newer threads now on the market. Check with your local needlework shop or department. Whatever type of thread you decide to use, be certain to buy at one time sufficient thread of the same dye lot to complete the doily you wish to make. It is often impossible to match shades later as dye lots vary.

For perfect results the number of stitches and rows should correspond with those indicated in the directions. Before starting your floral doily, make a small sample of the stitch, working with the suggested hook and desired thread. If your working tension is too tight or too loose, use a coarser or finer crochet hook to obtain the correct gauge.

When you have completed your doily, it should be washed and blocked. No matter how carefully you have worked, blocking will improve the doily's appearance and give it a "professional" look. Use a good neutral soap or detergent and make suds in warm water. Wash by squeezing the suds through the doily, but do not rub. Rinse two or three times in clear water and squeeze out the excess water. Starch lightly, if desired. Following the measurements given with the pattern, and using rust-proof pins, pin the article right side down on a well-padded surface. Be sure to pin out all picots, loops, scallops, etc., along the outside edges. When the doily is almost completely dry, press through a damp cloth with a moderately hot iron (do not rest the iron on the decorative, raised stitches). When thoroughly dry, remove the pins.

All of the stitches and abbreviations used in the projects in this book are explained on page 48.

New Pansy Doily

This doily may be made with any of the American Thread Company products listed below:

Material	Quantity		Size of Needle	Approx. Diameter of Doily
"STAR" Tatting Cotton Article 25	{	3 Balls White 2 Balls each Shaded Yellows and Shaded Lavenders 1 Ball Green	13 or 14	6 inches
or				
"STAR" Crochet Cotton Article 20, Size 30	{	1 Ball White 1 Ball each Shaded Yellows, Shaded Lavenders and Green	11 or 12	8 inches
or				
"STAR" Crochet Cotton Article 30, Size 30	{	2 Balls White 1 Ball each Shaded Yellows, Shaded Lavenders and Green	11 or 12	8 inches
or				
"GEM" Crochet Cotton Article 35, Size 30	{	1 Ball White 1 Ball each Shaded Yellows, Shaded Lavenders and Green	11 or 12	8 inches

Material	Quantity		Size of Needle	Approx. Diameter of Doily
or				
"SILLATEEN SANSIL" Article 102	{	2 Balls White 1 Ball each Shaded Yellows, Shaded Lavenders and Green	10	9 inches
or				
"DE LUXE" Crochet Cotton Article 346	{	1 Ball White 1 Ball each Shaded Yellows, Shaded Lavenders and Green	7	10 inches
or				
"STAR" Pearl Cotton Article 90, Size 5	{	3 Balls White 2 Balls each Shaded Yellows and Shaded Lavenders 1 Ball Green	7	10 inches

Plain Color may be used if desired.

With White ch 8, join to form a ring, ch 6, d c in ring, * ch 3, d c in ring, repeat from * 13 times, ch 3, join in 3rd st of ch.

2nd Row—Sl st into loop, ch 4, 2 tr c in same space, * ch 5, skip 1 loop, 3 tr c in next loop, repeat from * 6 times, ch 5, join in 4th st of ch.

3rd Row—Sl st to next tr c, ch 4, 2 tr c in same space, * ch 3, s c in next loop, ch 3, 3 tr c in center tr c of next tr c group, repeat from * 6 times, ch 3, s c in next loop, ch 3, join in 4th st of ch.

4th Row—Sl st to next tr c, ch 7, ** thread over needle twice, insert in next loop, pull through, thread over and work off 2 loops twice, * thread over needle twice, insert in same space, pull through, thread over and work off 2 loops twice, repeat from * once, repeat from ** once, thread over and work off all loops at one time (6 tr c cluster st), ch 7, s c in center tr c of next tr c group, ch 7, repeat from 1st ** all around in same manner ending row with s c in sl st.

5th Row—Ch 9, s c in next loop, * ch 7, s c in next loop, ch 5, 1 tr c in next s c, ch 5, s c in next loop, repeat from * 6 times, ch 7, s c in next loop, ch 2, d c in 4th st of ch.

6th Row—Ch 5, s c in next loop, ch 9, s c in next loop, ch 9, s c in next loop, repeat from beginning all around in same manner ending row with ch 4, d tr c (3 times over needle), in d c.

7th Row—Ch 3, 3 tr c, ch 3, 3 tr c (shell) in center st of next loop, ch 3, s c in next loop, ch 7, s c in next loop, repeat from beginning all around in same manner ending row with ch 3, d c in d tr c.

8th Row—Ch 8, s c in next loop, repeat from beginning all around ending row with ch 4, tr c in d c.

9th Row—Ch 9, s c in next loop, repeat from beginning all around ending row with ch 4, d tr c in tr c.

10th Row—Ch 4, shell in center st of next loop, ch 4, s c in next loop, ch 9, s c in next loop, ch 9, s c in next loop, repeat from beginning all around in same manner ending row with ch 4, d tr c in d tr c.

11th Row—Same as 8th row but ending row with tr c in d tr c.

12th Row—Same as 9th row.

13th Row—Ch 3, 2 d c in same space, * ch 6, 3 d c in center st of next loop, repeat from * all around, ch 6, join in 3rd st of ch.

14th Row—Sl st to next d c, ch 4, 2 tr c in same space, * ch 3, s c in next loop, ch 3, 3 tr c in center d c of next d c group, repeat from * all around in same manner, join in 3rd st of ch.

15th Row—Ch 7, 6 tr c cluster st over the next 2 loops, ch 7, s c in next loop, ch 5, s c in next loop, ch 7, 6 tr c cluster st over next 2 loops, ch 7, s c in center tr c of next tr c group, ch 7, 6 tr c cluster st over the next 2 loops, ch 7, s c in next loop, ch 5, s c in next loop, repeat from beginning all around in same manner, break thread.

PANSY—With Shaded Yellows ch 7, join to form a ring, ch 3 (counts as 1 d c), 2 d c in ring, * ch 7, 3 d c in ring, repeat from * 3 times, ch 7, join.

2nd Row—Sl st to loop, ch 3 (counts as 1 d c), work 15 more d c in loop, s c in center d c of next 3 d c group, * 16 d c in next loop, s c in center d c of next 3 d c group, repeat from * once (3 petals), ch 4, 12 d tr c (3 times around needle) with ch 1 between each d tr c in next loop, ch 1, 2 tr c with ch 1 between in same loop, ch 1, 2 d c with ch 1 between in same loop, s c in center d c of next 3 d c group, 2 d c with ch 1 between in next loop, ch 1, 2 tr c with ch 1 between in same loop, ch 1, 12 d tr c with ch 1 between each d tr c in same loop, ch 4, s c in center of next d c group, join, break thread. Work 7 more Shaded Yellow pansies and 8 Shaded Lavender pansies in same manner.

Attach Green in center st of 2nd loop to right of single cluster st, ** ch 4, * thread over needle twice, insert in same space, pull through, thread over and work off 2 loops twice, repeat from *, thread over and work off all loops at one time, ch 3, sl st in top of st just made for picot, ch 4, sl st in same space of loop, (leaf) ch 5, 2 d c in top of next cluster st, ch 1, sl st in center st of 2nd small petal of Lavender pansy, ch 1, 2 d c in same cluster st, ch 5, skip 1 loop, sl st in center st of next loop, leaf in same space, ch 7, s c in next cluster st, ch 4, sl st in 4th st of center small petal of Yellow pansy, ch 3, 2 d c in next s c, ch 1, sl st in center st of same petal of pansy, ch 1, 2 d c in same s c of doily, ch 3, skip 3 d c of same petal of pansy, sl st in next st, ch 4, s c in next cluster st, ch 7, skip 1 loop, sl st in center st of next loop, repeat from ** all around in same manner until all pansies are joined alternating Colors, break thread. Join White in s c between large petals at top of Yellow pansy, * ch 3, s c in next 1 ch loop, repeat from * 14 times, ch 3, s c in ch 4 loop of same pansy, ch 3, s c in 4 ch loop of large petal of Lavender pansy, work ch 3 loops across 2 large petals of pansy, ch 3, join the next Yellow pansy and continue until all pansies are joined.

Pond Lily Doily

This doily may be made with any of the American Thread Company products listed below:

Material	Quantity	Size of Needle	Diameter of Doily
"STAR" Tatting Cotton Article 25	3 Balls White / 2 Balls Shaded Yellows	13 or 14	6 inches
or			
"STAR" Crochet Cotton Article 20, Size 30	1 Ball White / 1 Ball Shaded Yellows	11 or 12	8 inches
or			
"STAR" Crochet Cotton Article 30, Size 30	1 Ball White / 1 Ball Shaded Yellows	11 or 12	8 inches
or			
"GEM" Crochet Cotton Article 35, Size 30	1 Ball White / 1 Ball Shaded Yellows	11 or 12	8 inches
or			
"SILLATEEN SANSIL" Article 102	1 Ball White / 1 Ball Shaded Yellows	10	9 inches
or			
"STAR" Rayon Crochet Article 700	1 Ball each White & Yellow	9 or 10	9 inches
or			
"DE LUXE" Crochet Cotton Article 346	1 Ball White / 1 Ball Shaded Yellows	7	10 inches
or			
"STAR" Pearl Cotton Article 90, Size 5	3 Balls White / 2 Balls Shaded Yellows	7 or 8	10 inches

Plain Color may be used if desired.

With Yellow, ch 6, join and work 2 s c in each st of ch, join.
2nd Row—Ch 4, 4 d c in same space, slip loop off hook, insert in 1st d c and pull loop through, * ch 3, 5 d c in next s c, sl loop off hook, insert in 1st d c and pull loop through (popcorn st), repeat from * 10 times, ch 3, join.
3rd Row—Ch 1 and work 3 s c in each ch 3 loop, join and work 1 more row of s c working into the back loop of st only.
5th Row—Ch 3 and work a popcorn st with ch 3 between each popcorn st in every other s c, join.
6th Row—Work 5 s c in each ch 3 increasing one st in row (91 s c), break thread.
PETAL—Join White and work 1 s c in each of the 1st 5 s c, ch 1, turn and work 2 rows of s c.
4th Row—Increase 1 st in 2nd s c, work across row and work 2 rows of s c even. Repeat the last 3 rows until there are 12 s c in row and work 11 rows even.
Next Row—Skip the 1st s c, 1 s c in each remaining s c. Repeat the last row until 4 sts remain, break thread.
Skip 2 s c around Yellow center and work a petal on **next** 5 sts. Work 11 more petals in same manner, break thread.
EDGE AND JOINING ROW—Attach Yellow to base of **one** petal and working into each row of side of petal, work 6 s c, ch 3, 6 s c, ch 4, * 6 s c, ch 5, repeat from * 3 times, 6 s c working the last 2 s c in 1st 2 s c on top of petal, ch 5 and work other side of petal to correspond, sl st to base of petal, sl st across next 2 s c of center of flower and into base of next petal work 6 s c in 2nd petal, ch 2, join to corresponding picot of previous petal (to join slip loop off hook, insert in ch of opposite picot and **pull** loop through), ch 2, 6 s c, ch 2, join to next picot, ch 2, 6 s c, ch 3, join to next picot, ch 3, 6 s c, ch 3, join **to** next picot, ch 3 and complete 2nd petal same as 1st petal. Join all petals in same manner joining last petal to previous and 1st petal, sl st to base of petal and across **next** 2 s c of center, join, break thread.

MAGNOLIA GARDENS

It has the delicacy and elegance you associate with fine things—use
it on your choicest heirloom table—under your favorite bric-a-brac.

MATERIALS: For best results use—

CLARK'S O.N.T. OR J & P. COATS

BEST SIX CORD MERCERIZED CROCHET, Size 30:

SMALL BALL:

CLARK'S O.N.T.—*5 balls of White or Ecru. or 7 balls*
OR *of any color.*

J. & P. COATS—*4 balls of White or Ecru. or 5 balls*
of any color.

BIG BALL:

CLARK'S O.N.T.—*2 balls of White or Ecru.*
OR

J. & P. COATS—*2 balls of White or Ecru, or 3 balls*
of any color.

MILWARD'S *steel crochet hook No. 10 or 11.*

Completed runner measures about 11½ x 23 inches.

GAUGE: Motif measures about 3 inches in diameter.

FIRST MOTIF... Starting at center, ch 10, join with
sl st. **1st rnd:** 24 s c in ring; join. **2nd rnd:** Ch 4 (to
count as d c and ch-1), * d c in next s c, ch 1. Repeat
from * around; join (24 sps). **3rd rnd:** S c in sl st,
* s c in next sp, s c in next d c. Repeat from * around;
join. **4th rnd:** S c in each s c; join. **5th rnd:** * Ch 10,
skip 3 s c, s c in next s c. Repeat from * around

(12 loops). **6th rnd:** 13 s c in each loop. **7th rnd:**
Sl st in 4 s c, s c in next s c, ch 5 (to count as tr and
ch-1), tr in next 4 s c with ch-1 between each tr;
* skip 4 s c on this loop and 4 s c on next loop, tr
in next 5 s c with ch-1 between each tr. Repeat from
* around. Join to 4th st of ch-5. **8th rnd:** S c in sl st,
* s c in next sp, s c in next tr, ch 3, s c in 3rd ch from
hook (p); ** s c in next sp, s c in next tr, p. Repeat
from ** once more, s c in next sp, s c in next 2 tr.
Repeat from * around. Fasten off.

SECOND MOTIF... Work 7 rnds as for first motif. **8th
rnd:** S c in sl st, * s c in next sp, s c in next tr, p,
s c in next sp, s c in next tr, ch 1, join to center p of
any 3-p group on first motif, ch 1 and complete p on
2nd motif, s c in next sp and work rnd as for 1st motif.
Join 4 x 8 motifs, leaving two 3-p groups free between joinings.

FILL-IN LACE... Starting at center, ch 6, join. **1st rnd:**
16 s c in ring; join. **2nd rnd:** Ch 8, sl st in center p of
any free p-group between motifs, * ch 8, skip 1 s c,
s c in next s c on ring, ch 8, sl st in center p of next
free p-group. Repeat from * around, ending with
ch 8, skip 1 s c, s c in 1st s c made on ring. Fasten off.

African Violet Ruffle Doily

This doily may be made with any of the American Thread Company products listed below:

Material	Quantity	Size of Needle	Approx. diameter of Doily
"STAR" Tatting Cotton Article 25 or	10 Balls White 1 Ball each Yellow, Lavender and Pink	13 or 14	6½ inches without ruffle
"STAR" Crochet Cotton Article 20, Size 30 or	2 Balls White 1 Ball each Yellow, Lavender and Pink	11 or 12	8½ inches without ruffle
"STAR" Crochet Cotton Article 30, Size 30 or	5 Balls White 1 Ball each Yellow, Lavender and Pink	11 or 12	8½ inches without ruffle
"GEM" Crochet Cotton Article 35, Size 30 or	2 Balls White 1 Ball each Yellow, Lavender and Pink	11 or 12	8½ inches without ruffle
"SILLATEEN SANSIL" Article 102 or	5 Balls White 1 Ball each Yellow, Lavender and Pink	10	9½ inches without ruffle
"DE LUXE" Crochet Cotton Article 346 or	2 Balls White 1 Ball each Yellow, Lavender and Pink	7	10½ inches without ruffle
"STAR" Pearl Cotton Article 90, Size 5	10 Balls White 2 Balls each Yellow, Lavender and Pink	7	10½ inches without ruffle

Shaded Color may be used if desired

With White ch 8, join to form a ring and work 16 s c in ring, join.

2nd Row—Ch 5, skip 1 s c, s c in next s c, repeat from beginning 6 times, ch 2, d c in joining (this brings thread in position for next row).

3rd Row—2 s c in same loop, * ch 5, 2 s c in next loop, repeat from * 6 times, ch 1, tr c in 1st s c.

4th Row—3 s c in same loop, * ch 7, 3 d c in center st of next loop, ch 7, 3 s c in next loop, repeat from * twice, ch 7, 3 d c in center st of next loop, ch 3, d c in 1st s c.

5th Row—Ch 9, s c in next loop, ch 3, 3 tr c in next d c, ch 3, skip 1 d c, 3 tr c in next d c, ch 3, s c in next loop, repeat from beginning twice, ch 9, s c in next loop, ch 3, 3 tr c in next d c, ch 3, skip 1 d c, 3 tr c in next d c, ch 3, sl st in d c.

6th Row—Sl st to center of loop, ch 6, d c in same space, * ch 5, 3 tr c in next tr c, ch 3, skip 1 tr c, 3 tr c in next tr c, ch 3, 3 tr c in next tr c, ch 3, skip 1 tr c, 3 tr c in next tr c, ch 5, 2 d c with ch 3 between in center st of next loop, repeat from * twice, ch 5, 3 tr c in next tr c, ch 3, skip 1 tr c, 3 tr c in next tr c, ch 3, 3 tr c in next tr c, ch 3, skip 1 tr c, 3 tr c in next tr c, ch 2, d c in 3rd st of ch.

7th Row—Ch 7, cluster st in center st of next loop (cluster st: thread over needle twice, insert in st, pull through, thread over and work off 2 loops twice, * thread over needle twice, insert in same space, pull through, thread over and work off 2 loops twice, repeat from * twice, thread over and work off all loops at one time), ch 7, s c in next loop, repeat from beginning all around ending row with ch 2, d tr c in d c (12 cluster sts).

8th Row—Ch 7, s c in next loop, repeat from beginning all around ending row with ch 2, tr c in d tr c.

9th Row—2 s c in same loop, * ch 7, 3 d c in center st of next loop, ch 7, 2 s c in next loop, repeat from * 10 times,

8

ch 7, 3 d c in center st of next loop, ch 2, d tr c in 1st s c.

10th Row—Ch 9, s c in next loop, ch 3, 3 tr c in next d c, ch 3, skip 1 d c, 3 tr c in next loop, ch 3, s c in next loop, repeat from beginning all around in same manner, ending row with sl st in d tr c.

11th Row—Sl st to center of loop, * ch 7, s c in next loop, ch 7, cluster st in center st of next loop, ch 7, s c in next loop, ch 7, s c in next loop, repeat from * all around in same manner ending row with ch 3, d c in last sl st.

12th Row—Ch 7, s c in next loop, repeat from beginning all around ending row with ch 2, tr c in d c.

13th Row—Ch 3, 3 d c in center st of next loop, ch 3, s c in next loop, ch 7, 2 s c in next loop, ch 7, s c in next loop, repeat from beginning all around ending row with ch 3, d c in tr c.

14th Row—Ch 5, 3 tr c in next d c, ch 3, skip 1 d c, 3 tr c in next d c, ch 5, skip 1 loop, s c in next loop, ch 7, s c in next loop, repeat from beginning all around ending row with ch 3, tr c in d c.

15th Row—Ch 7, s c in next loop, ch 7, cluster st in center st of next loop, * ch 7, s c in next loop, repeat from * once, repeat from beginning all around ending row with ch 3, tr c in tr c.

16th Row—Ch 9, s c in next loop, repeat from beginning all around ending row with ch 4, d tr c in tr c.

17th Row—Ch 7, 3 d c in center st of next loop, ch 7, s c in next loop, * ch 9, s c in next loop, repeat from * once, repeat from beginning all around in same manner ending row with ch 4, d tr c in d tr c.

18th Row—Ch 9, s c in next loop, ch 5, 3 tr c in next d c, ch 3, skip 1 d c, 3 tr c in next d c, ch 5, s c in next loop, * ch 9, s c in next loop, repeat from * once, repeat from beginning all around in same manner ending row with ch 4, d tr c in d tr c.

19th Row—* Ch 9, s c in next loop, repeat from * once, * * ch 7, cluster st in center st of next loop, ch 7, s c in next loop, * ch 9, s c in next loop, repeat from * 3 times, repeat from * * all around in same manner ending row with ch 4, d tr c in d tr c.

20th Row—Ch 7, s c in next loop, repeat from beginning all around ending row with ch 3, d c in d tr c.

21st Row—Ch 7, tr c in same space, * ch 5, s c in next loop, ch 5, 2 tr c with ch 3 between in center st of next loop, repeat from * all around ending row with ch 2, d c in 3rd st of ch.

22nd Row—Ch 5, cluster st in center st of next loop, ch 5, s c in next loop, ch 5, s c in next loop, repeat from beginning all around in same manner ending row with ch 5, sl st in d c.

23rd Row—Sl st to top of next cluster st, * ch 7, skip 1 loop, cluster st in center st of next loop, ch 7, s c in top of next cluster st, repeat from * all around ending row with ch 3, d c in last sl st.

24th Row—* Ch 9, s c in next loop, repeat from * all around ending row with ch 4, d tr c in d c.

25th Row—Same as 20th row, ending row with ch 4, d c in d tr c.

26th Row—Ch 10, s c in next loop, * ch 10, s c in same loop, repeat from * once, repeat from beginning all around ending row with ch 5, d tr c in d c.

Next 9 Rows—Ch 10, s c in next loop, repeat from beginning all around ending each row with ch 5, d tr c in d tr c, break thread.

FLOWER—With Pink, ch 2, 5 s c in 2nd st from hook, join.

Next Row—Ch 4, * thread over needle twice, insert in same space and work off 2 loops twice, repeat from * once, thread over and work off all loops at one time, ch 3, sl st in same space, sl st to next s c, repeat from beginning 4 times (5 petals), break thread. Work 13 more Pink flowers and 14 Lavender flowers. With Yellow, using a double strand of thread embroider a French knot in the center of each flower leaving ends long enough to tie on doily.

DIRECTIONS FOR STARCHING DOILY —

STARCH: Dissolve ¼ cup starch in ½ cup of cold water. Boil slowly over a low flame, as it thickens stir in gradually about 1¼ cups of cold water. Boil, stirring constantly until starch clears. This makes a thick pasty mixture. As soon as starch is cool enough to handle, dip doily and squeeze starch through it thoroughly. Wring out extra starch. The doily should be wet with starch but there should be none in the spaces. Pin center of doily in position according to size and leave until thoroughly dry. If steam iron is used, iron ruffle after it is dry. If regular iron is used, dampen ruffle slightly before pressing. Pin folds of ruffle in position and leave until thoroughly dry.

After doily is dry tie flowers over loops of doily as illustrated alternating the Colors.

Irish Rose Doily

This doily may be made with any of the American Thread Company products listed below:

Material	Quantity		Size of Needle	Approx. Diameter of Doily
"STAR" Tatting Cotton Article 25	{	2 Balls each White, Shaded Pinks and Green	13 or 14	5¾ inches
or				
"STAR" Crochet Cotton Article 20, Size 30	{	1 Ball each White, Shaded Pinks and Green	11 or 12	7¾ inches
or				
"STAR" Crochet Cotton Article 30, Size 30	{	1 Ball each White, Shaded Pinks and Green	11 or 12	7¾ inches
or				
"GEM" Crochet Cotton Article 35, Size 30	{	1 Ball each White, Shaded Pinks and Green	11 or 12	7¾ inches
or				
"SILLATEEN SANSIL" Article 102	{	1 Ball each White, Shaded Pinks and Green	10	8¾ inches
or				
"DE LUXE" Crochet Cotton Article 346	{	1 Ball each White, Shaded Pinks and Green	7	9¾ inches
or				
"STAR" Pearl Cotton Article 90, Size 5	{	2 Balls each White, Shaded Pinks and Green	7	9¾ inches

Plain Color may be used if desired.

With White ch 7, join to form a ring, ch 3, d c in ring, ch 3 and work 7 cluster sts with ch 3 between each cluster st in ring, (cluster st: * thread over needle, insert in ring, pull through, thread over and pull through 2 loops, repeat from * once, thread over and pull through all loops at one time) ch 3, join in 3rd st of ch.

10

2nd Row—Ch 1 and work 4 s c over each loop, join.

3rd Row—Ch 8, d c in same space, skip 4 s c, * 1 d c, ch 5, 1 d c in space over next cluster st of previous row, repeat from * all around, join in 3rd st of ch.

4th Row—Ch 1 and * work 6 s c over next loop, s c in center of next 2 d c, repeat from * all around, join.

5th Row—Sl st in each of the next 2 s c, ch 18, s c in 2nd st from hook and work 19 s c over balance of ch, 1 sl st in each of the next 2 s c of circle, ** ch 1, turn and working in back loop of st only for entire scroll, 1 s c in each of the next 19 s c on scroll, ch 3, turn, 1 s c in 3rd ch from hook, 1 s c in each of the next 5 s c, * ch 1, turn, 1 s c in each of the next 4 s c, ch 3, turn, 1 s c in 3rd ch from hook, 1 s c in each of the next 4 s c, 1 s c in each of the next 2 s c on side of scroll, repeat from * 6 times, 1 sl st in each of the next 5 s c of circle working through both loops, ch 17, turn, sl st in 3rd picot from bottom of scroll just completed, ch 1, turn and work 20 s c over ch, 1 sl st in each of the next 2 s c of circle working through both loops, repeat from ** until 7 scrolls have been completed. Work another scroll, joining the 3rd picot from bottom to tip of 1st scroll made and complete scroll, then work 1 sl st in each of the next 3 s c of circle, join, break thread.

6th Row—Attach thread in 2nd free picot of any scroll, s c in same space, ** ch 6, s c in next free picot, * ch 6, s c in next free picot, repeat from * once, ch 6, skip 1st picot of next scroll, s c in next free picot, repeat from ** 6 times, ending row with * ch 6, s c in next picot, repeat from * twice, ch 2, tr c in 1st s c, this brings thread in position for next row.

7th Row—Ch 3, s c in same space, * ch 6, 1 s c, ch 3, 1 s c in next loop, repeat from * all around ending row with ch 3, tr c in tr c.

8th Row—Ch 7, s c in next ch 6 loop, repeat from beginning all around ending row with ch 3, tr c in tr c.

9th Row—Same as 7th row.

10th Row—Ch 9, s c in next loop, repeat from beginning all around ending row with ch 3, d tr c in tr c.

11th Row—Ch 3, 2 d c in same space leaving last loop of each d c on hook, thread over and pull through all loops at one time, ch 5, cluster st in same space (cluster st: thread over needle, insert in space, pull through, thread over and work off 2 loops, * thread over needle, insert in same space, pull through, thread over and work off 2 loops, repeat from * once, thread over and pull through all loops at one time), * ch 7, s c in next loop, ch 7, 2 cluster sts with ch 5 between in next loop, repeat from * all around ending row with ch 7, s c in next loop, ch 7, join.

12th Row—Sl st into loop between cluster sts, ch 3 (counts as part of 1st cluster st) and work 4 cluster sts with ch 3 between each cluster st in same loop, * ch 3, s c in next loop, ch 7, s c in next loop, ch 3, 4 cluster sts with ch 3 between each cluster st in loop between next 2 cluster sts, repeat from * all around ending row with ch 3, s c in next loop, ch 7, s c in next loop, ch 3, join, break thread.

ROSES—With Shaded Pinks, ch 5, join to form a ring, ch 6, d c in ring, * ch 3, d c in ring, repeat from * 3 times, ch 3, join in 3rd st of ch.

2nd Row—Over each loop, work 1 s c, 1 s d c, 3 d c, 1 s d c, 1 s c, (s d c: thread over needle, insert in st, pull through, thread over and pull through all loops at one time).

3rd Row—* Ch 5, s c in back of work between the s c of next 2 petals, repeat from * all around.

4th Row—Over each loop, work 1 s c, 1 s d c, 5 d c, 1 s d c, 1 s c.

5th Row—* Ch 7, sl st in back of work between next 2 petals, repeat from * all around.

6th Row—1 s c, 1 d c, 7 tr c, 1 d c, 1 s c in next loop, 1 s c, 1 d c, 4 tr c in next loop, ch 1, then holding doily wrong side toward you, sl st in ch 7 loop between 2 cluster st groups, ch 1, turn, sl st in top of tr c of petal, 3 tr c, 1 d c, 1 s c in same loop of rose, 1 s c, 1 d c, 7 tr c, 1 d c, 1 s c in each of the next 4 loops of rose, join, break thread.

LEAF—With Green, ch 13, 1 s c in 2nd st from hook, 1 s c in each of the next 10 sts of ch, 3 s c in next st of ch, working on other side of ch, work 1 s c in each of the next 8 sts, ch 3, turn, picking up the back loop of st only throughout, 1 s c in each of the next 9 s c, 3 s c in next s c, 1 s c in each of the next 7 s c, * ch 3, turn, 1 s c in each of the next 8 s c, 3 s c in next s c, 1 s c in each of the next 7 s c, repeat from * 4 times, ch 1, turn, sl st in center st of 3rd petal made of previous rose, ch 1, turn, 1 s c in each of the next 8 s c of leaf, 2 s c in next s c, ch 1 and having wrong side of doily toward you, sl st in next ch 7 loop of doily, ch 1, s c in same st of leaf, 1 s c in each of the next 7 s c of leaf, ch 3, turn, sl st in each of the next 3 s c, break thread.

Work 7 more roses and 7 more leaves, alternating roses and leaves, joining 1st petal of rose to last picot of previous leaf and 2nd petal of rose to next ch 7 loop of doily. Join all leaves same as 1st leaf, joining last leaf to 1st petal of 1st rose to correspond.

11

Daisy Doily

This doily may be made with any of the American Thread Company products listed below:

Material	Quantity	Size of Needle	Approx. Diameter of Doily
"STAR" Tatting Cotton Article 25	2 Balls White 3 Balls Yellow	13 or 14	6½ inches
or			
"STAR" Crochet Cotton Article 20, Size 30	1 Ball each White and Yellow	11 or 12	8½ inches
or			
"STAR" Crochet Cotton Article 30, Size 30	1 Ball White 2 Balls Yellow	11 or 12	8½ inches
or			
"GEM" Crochet Cotton Article 35, Size 30	1 Ball each White and Yellow	11 or 12	8½ inches
or			
"SILLATEEN SANSIL" Article 102	1 Ball White 2 Balls Yellow	10	9½ inches
or			
"DE LUXE" Crochet Cotton Article 346	1 Ball each White and Yellow	7	10½ inches
or			
"STAR" Pearl Cotton Article 90, Size 5	2 Balls White 3 Balls Yellow	7	10½ inches

Shaded Colors may be used if desired.

With Yellow ch 2, 5 s c in 2nd st from hook.

2nd Row—Working around, work 2 s c in each s c (10 s c), join.

3rd Row—Ch 1, 1 s c in each s c, break Yellow.

Attach White, * ch 10, s c in 2nd st from hook, 1 s d c in next st of ch (s d c: thread over needle, insert in stitch, pull through, thread over and work off all loops at one time), 1 d c in each of the next 7 sts of ch, s c in next s c, repeat from * 9 times (10 petals), break White.

1st Row—Attach Yellow at top of petal, * ch 5, thread over needle, insert in 3rd st from top on side of same petal, pull through, thread over and work off 2 loops, thread over needle, insert in 3rd st from top of next petal, pull through, thread over and work off 2 loops, thread over and work off all loops at one time, ch 5, s c in top of same petal, repeat from * all around ending row with ch 2, d c in same space as beginning (this brings thread in position for next row).

2nd Row—Ch 3, s c in same space, * ch 5, s c in next loop, ch 3, s c in same space (picot), repeat from * all around ending row with ch 2, d c in same space as beginning.

3rd Row—* Ch 6, s c in next loop, repeat from * all around ending row with ch 3, tr c in d c.

4th Row—Ch 3, s c in same space, * ch 6, s c in next loop, ch 3, s c in same space, repeat from * all around ending row with ch 3, tr c in tr c.

5th Row—Ch 7, d c in same space, * ch 5, 1 d c, ch 4, 1 d c in next loop, repeat from * all around ending row with ch 5, sl st in 3rd st of ch 7.

6th Row—Sl st into loop, ch 3, 2 d c in same space, * ch 3, s c in next loop, ch 3, 3 d c in next loop, repeat from * all around ending row with ch 3, s c in next loop, ch 3, join.

7th Row—Ch 3, d c in same space, d c in next d c, 2 d c in next d c, * ch 4, s c in next s c, ch 4, 2 d c in next d c, d c in next d c, 2 d c in next d c, repeat from * all around ending row with ch 4, s c in next s c, ch 4, join.

8th Row—Same as last row but working 1 d c in each of the 5 d c in each d c group.

9th Row—Sl st to center d c of group, ch 6, d c in same space, * ch 4, d c in next s c, ch 4, 1 d c, ch 3, 1 d c (shell) in center d c of next d c group, repeat from * all around ending row with ch 4, d c in next s c, ch 4, join in 3rd st of ch.

10th Row—Sl st into loop, ch 6, d c in same space, * ch 5, s c in single d c, ch 5, 1 d c, ch 3, 1 d c in center of next shell, repeat from * all around ending row with ch 5, s c in next d c, ch 5, join in 3rd st of ch.

11th Row—Sl st into loop, ch 6, d c in same space, * ch 5, d c in next s c, ch 5, 1 d c, ch 3, 1 d c in next shell, repeat from * all around in same manner ending row to correspond, join.

12th Row—Sl st into loop, ch 6, d c in same space, * ch 6, s c in next single d c, ch 6, 1 d c, ch 3, 1 d c in next shell, repeat from * all around in same manner ending row to correspond, join in 3rd st of ch.

13th Row—Sl st into loop, ch 6, d c in same space, * ch 7, d c in next s c, ch 7, shell in next shell, repeat from * all around in same manner ending row to correspond, join in 3rd st of ch.

14th Row—Sl st into loop, ch 3, 2 d c in same space keeping last loop of each d c on hook, thread over and pull through all loops at one time, ch 4, cluster st in same space (cluster st: thread over needle, insert in space, pull through and work off 2 loops, * thread over needle, in-sert in same space, pull through and work off 2 loops, repeat from * once, thread over and work off all loops at one time), * ch 7, s c in next d c, ch 4, s c in same space for picot, ch 7, 2 cluster sts with ch 4 between in next shell, repeat from * all around ending row with ch 7, s c in next d c, ch 4, s c in same space, ch 7, join, break thread.

DAISY—Work 1st 2 rows same as center flower, break Yellow. Attach White, ch 8 and with wrong side of doily toward you, s c in ch 4 loop of doily between the 2 cluster sts, turn, s c in 2nd ch from hook, 1 s d c in each of the next 6 sts of ch, s c in next s c of Yellow center, ch 8, turn, s c in next picot of doily, turn, s c in 2nd ch from hook, 1 s d c in each of the next 6 sts of ch, s c in next s c of Yellow center, ch 8, turn, s c in next ch 4 loop be-tween next 2 cluster sts, turn, s c in 2nd ch from hook, 1 s d c in each of the next 6 sts of ch, s c in next s c of Yellow center, then work 7 more petals to complete flower in same manner but do not join.

2nd Flower—Work Yellow center same as previous flower. Attach White, ch 8, s c in 4th petal of previous flower, s c in 2nd ch from hook, 1 s d c in each of the next 6 sts of ch, s c in next s c of Yellow center, work another petal joining it in same space of doily as 3rd petal of previous flower, join 3rd petal in next picot of doily and join 4th petal to next ch 4 loop between next 2 cluster sts, com-plete flower same as 1st flower having 10 petals.

Work 18 more flowers joining same as 2nd flower and join last flower to corresponding petal of 1st flower.

Forget-Me-Not Doily

This doily may be made with any of the American Thread Company products listed below:

Material	Quantity	Size of Needle	Approx. Diameter of Doily
"STAR" Tatting Cotton Article 25	2 Balls White, 3 Balls Shaded Blues 2 Balls Yellow	13 or 14	7 inches
or			
"STAR" Crochet Cotton Article 20, Size 30	1 Ball each White Shaded Blues and Yellow	11 or 12	9 inches
or			
"STAR" Crochet Cotton Article 30, Size 30	1 Ball each White and Yellow 2 Balls Shaded Blues	11 or 12	9 inches
or			
"GEM" Crochet Cotton Article 35, Size 30	1 Ball each White Shaded Blues and Yellow	11 or 12	9 inches
or			
"SILLATEEN SANSIL" Article 102	1 Ball each White and Yellow 2 Balls Shaded Blues	10	10 inches
or			
"DE LUXE" Crochet Cotton Article 346	1 Ball each White Shaded Blues and Yellow	7	11 inches
or			
"STAR" Pearl Cotton Article 90, Size 5	2 Balls White 4 Balls Shaded Blues 1 Ball Yellow	7	11 inches

Plain Color may be used if desired.

With White ch 8, join to form a ring, ch 1 and work 12 s c in ring, join.

2nd Row—Ch 5, d c in next s c, * ch 2, d c in next s c, repeat from * all around, ch 2, join in 3rd st of ch.

3rd Row—Ch 1 and work 3 s c over each loop, join.

4th Row—* Ch 6, s c in space over the d c of previous row, repeat from * all around ending row with ch 3, tr c in same space as beginning (this brings thread in position for next row).

5th Row—* Ch 6, s c in next loop, repeat from * all around.

6th Row—Sl st into loop, ch 1 and work 3 s c in same space, * ch 6, 3 s c in next loop, repeat from * all around, ending row with ch 2, d tr c in the sl st.

7th Row—Ch 3, 2 d c in same loop, * ch 3, skip 1 s c, d c in next s c, ch 3, 3 d c in next loop, repeat from * all around ending row with ch 3, skip 1 s c, d c in next s c, ch 3, join.

8th Row—Ch 3, d c in same space, 1 d c in next d c, 2 d c in next d c, * ch 3, d c in next single d c, ch 3, 2 d c in next d c, d c in next d c, 2 d c in next d c, repeat from * all around ending row with ch 3, d c in next single d c, ch 3, join.

9th and 10th Rows—Same as last row but having 2 more d c in each solid section of each row.

11th Row—Sl st to next d c, ch 3, 1 d c in each of the next 6 d c, * ch 3, d c in next loop, ch 3, d c in next loop, ch 3, 1 d c in each of the center 7 d c of next d c group, repeat from * all around ending row with ch 3, d c in next loop, ch 3, d c in next loop, ch 3, join.

12th Row—Sl st to next d c, ch 3, 1 d c in each of the next 4 d c, * ch 3, d c in next loop, ch 3, d c in next loop, ch 3, d c in next loop, ch 3, 1 d c in each of the center 5 d c of next d c group, repeat from * all around ending row to correspond, ch 3, join.

13th Row—Sl st to next d c, ch 3, 1 d c in each of the next 2 d c, * ch 3, d c in next loop, ch 3, d c in next loop, ch 3, d c in next loop, ch 3, d c in next loop, ch 3, 1 d c in each of the 3 center d c of next d c group, repeat from * all around ending row to correspond, ch 3, join.

14th Row—Sl st to next d c, ch 6, d c in next loop, * ch 3, d c in next loop, repeat from * 3 times, ** ch 3, d c in center d c of next d c group, * ch 3, d c in next loop, repeat from * 4 times, repeat from ** all around ending row to correspond, ch 3, join in 3rd st of ch.

15th Row—Ch 1 and work 4 s c over each loop, join.

16th Row—* Ch 6, s c in space over the next d c of previous row, repeat from * all around ending row with ch 3, d c in same space as beginning.

17th Row—* Ch 6, s c in next loop, repeat from * all around ending row with ch 3, d c in d c.

18th Row—Same as last row but ending row with ch 6, s c in d c.

19th Row—Ch 1 and work 5 s c over each loop, join, break thread.

Flower: With Yellow, ch 6, join to form a ring, * ch 4, s c in ring, repeat from * 5 times (6 loops), break Yellow. Attach Shaded Blues in loop, ch 4, 2 tr c in same loop, ch 1 and with wrong side of doily toward you, sl st in center st of any scallop of doily, ch 1, turn, sl st in same tr c of flower, 1 tr c in same loop of flower, ch 4, sl st in same loop of flower, sl st in next loop of center of flower, ch 4, 2 tr c in same space, ch 1, sl st in center st of next scallop of doily, ch 1, turn, sl st in top of same tr c of flower, 1 tr c in same loop of flower, ch 4, sl st in same loop of flower, * sl st in next loop of center of flower, ch 4, 3 tr c in same space, ch 4, sl st in same space, repeat from * 3 times, join (6 petals), break Blue. Work a 2nd flower joining side petal to side petal of 1st flower, skip 1 scallop on doily and join next 2 petals to next 2 scallops of doily. Work 22 more flowers in same manner joining same as previous flowers and having 2 petals free on top of each flower joining last flower to 1st flower at side petal.

2nd Row of Flowers—Work center same as 1st row of flowers. Attach Shaded Blues in loop, ch 4, 3 tr c in same space, ch 4, sl st in same space, sl st in next loop of center, ch 4, 2 tr c in same space, ch 1 and with wrong side of doily toward you, sl st in 2nd free petal of any flower, ch 1, turn, sl st in top of tr c just made, tr c in same loop of center, ch 4, sl st in same space, sl st in next loop, ch 4, 2 tr c in same loop, ch 1, sl st in 1st free petal of next flower, ch 1, turn, sl st in top of tr c just made, tr c in same loop of center, ch 4, sl st in same space, then complete remaining 3 petals same as other flowers.

2nd Flower—Work center same as 1st flower. Attach Shaded Blues in loop, ch 4, 2 tr c in same space, ch 3, sl st in center st of side petal of previous flower, ch 3, turn, sl st in top of tr c just made, tr c in same space, ch 4, sl st in same space, sl st in next loop of center and join next 2 petals to previous row of flowers same as 1st flower, then complete remaining petals of flower same as 1st flower. Work 22 more flowers and join same as 2nd flower joining the side petal of last flower made to side petal of 1st flower.

Above:
MARIPOSA

Left:
NOSEGAY

WHETHER you find a smart runner on the hall table, or a dainty doily elsewhere, you know the woman who uses them has that certain knack of making a home charming.

MARIPOSA

MATERIALS: For best results use—
  CLARK'S O.N.T. OR J. & P. COATS
 BEST SIX CORD MERCERIZED CROCHET, Size 30:
SMALL BALL:
CLARK'S O.N.T.—*4 balls of White or Ecru, or 6 balls*
  OR   *of any color.*
J. & P. COATS—*3 balls of White or Ecru, or 4 balls*
     of any color.
BIG BALL:
CLARK'S O.N.T.—*2 balls of White or Ecru.*
  OR
J. & P. COATS—*2 balls of White, Ecru, or any color.*
MILWARD'S *steel crochet hook No. 10.*
Completed runner measures about 12½ x 25 inches.
GAUGE: 5 sps make 1 inch; 5 rows make 1 inch.

Starting at bottom of chart, make a chain 15 inches long (15 ch sts to 1 inch). **1st row:** D c in 8th ch from hook; (ch 2, skip 2 ch, d c in next ch) 10 times— *11 sps made.* * D c in next 15 ch (5 bls made). Make 7 sps. Repeat from * 2 more times; 5 bls, 11 sps. Cut off remaining chain. Ch 5, turn. **2nd row:** D c in next d c (sp); 2 d c in next sp, d c in next d c—*bl made over sp;* make 9 bls over next 9 sps, * 5 sps, 7 bls. Repeat from * 2 more times, 5 sps, 10 bls, 1 sp. Ch 5, turn. Starting at 3rd row, follow chart until 11th row is completed. Ch 3, turn. **12th row:** D c in next 2 ch, d c in next d c (1 bl); 1 sp, 1 bl, 4 sps, and follow chart to end of row. Starting at 13th row, follow chart to top (63rd row—center of runner). Then reverse design and work back from 62nd row to 1st row. Fasten off.
Block to given measurements.

THERE ARE 10 SPACES BETWEEN HEAVY LINES

START HERE

NOSEGAY

MATERIALS: For best results use—
  CLARK'S O.N.T. OR J. & P. COATS
 BEST SIX CORD MERCERIZED CROCHET, Size 70:
SMALL BALL:
CLARK'S O.N.T. OR J. & P. COATS—*1 ball of White*
      or Ecru.
MILWARD'S *steel crochet hook No. 14.*
Completed doily measures about 10 inches in diameter.

MOTIF... Ch 10, join with sl st. **1st rnd:** Ch 7 (to count as d c and ch-4), * d c in ring, ch 4. Repeat from * 4 more times. Sl st in 3rd st of ch-7 first made (6 sps). **2nd rnd:** In each sp around make s c, half d c, 5 d c, half d c and s c. Sl st in sl st (6 petals). **3rd rnd:** * Ch 5, insert hook between next 2 petals from back of work and bring it out in following sp; thread over and draw loop through; thread over and draw through both loops on hook. Repeat from * 5 more times. **4th rnd:** Same as 2nd rnd, making 7 d c (instead of 5 d c) in center part of each petal. **5th rnd:** Same as 3rd rnd. **6th rnd:** Ch 3 (to count as d c), 11 d c in next ch-5 loop, 12 d c in each loop around. Sl st in 3rd st of ch-3 first made. **7th rnd:** Ch 11 (to count as tr and ch-7), skip 5 d c, tr between this and next d c (5th and 6th d c), * ch 7, skip 6 d c, tr between this and next d c (6th and 7th d c). Repeat from * around, ending with ch 7, sl st in 4th ch of ch-11 first made (12 sps). **8th rnd:** Ch 1, * 9 s c in sp, s c in next tr. Repeat from * around; join. **9th rnd:** Ch 12, sl st in 2nd ch from hook and in each ch across; sl st in sl st. * Ch 5, turn, skip 2 sts, d c in next st; (ch 2, skip 2 sts, d c in next st) 3 times. Repeat from * 3 more times (a square completed). ** Ch 11, s c in s c directly over next tr below, ch 5, turn; skip 2 sts, d c in next st, ch 2, skip 2 sts, d c in next st and complete a square as before. Repeat from ** around (12 squares). Join with sl st to tip of first ch-12 made. **10th rnd:** * 2 s c in next sp, s c in next st, 2 s c in next sp, s c in next st, ch 3, s c in 3rd ch from hook (p); 2 s c in next sp, s c in next st, 3 s c in next sp, p, 2 s c in same sp, s c in next st, 2 s c in next sp, s c in next st, p, 2 s c in next sp, s c in next st, 2 s c in next sp. Repeat from * around. Join and fasten off.

Make 6 more motifs. Place these 6 motifs around 1st motif, and sew together 2 points of each motif to 2 points of center motif. Join adjacent motifs at 2 corresponding points in same manner.

17

Crochet These Lovelies for Vanity's Sake!

Open beauty secret . . . give your bedroom a bit of glamour with these adorable crochet ideas.

Flowerstrewn

MATERIALS:

CLARK'S O.N.T. or J. & P. COATS BEST SIX CORD MERCERIZED CROCHET, size 30:

SMALL BALL:
CLARK'S O.N.T.—8 balls,
OR
J. & P. COATS —5 balls of White or Ecru, or 7 balls of any color.

BIG BALL:
J. & P. COATS —3 balls of White or Ecru, or 4 balls of any color.

Steel crochet hook No. 10 or 11.

Completed runner measures 14 x 31 inches when blocked.

GAUGE: Each motif measures 2¾ inches in diameter.

FIRST MOTIF . . . Starting at center, ch 10. Join. **1st rnd:** (Sc in ring, ch 5) 6 times. Sl st in 1st sc made. **2nd rnd:** In each loop make sc, h dc, 5 dc, h dc and sc (6 petals). **3rd rnd:** * Ch 5, insert hook in next loop (from back of work) and in following loop (from right of work), thread over and draw loop through, thread over and draw through both loops on hook. Repeat from * around until 6 loops are completed. **4th rnd:** Work petals as before, making 7 (instead of 5) dc in each petal. **5th rnd:** Sl st in 1st 3 sts of next petal, sc in next st, * ch 5, sc in 3rd st from hook (p made), ch 3, p, ch 2, skip 3 sts, sc in next st, ch 2, p, ch 3, p, ch 2, skip 3 sts of next petal, sc in next st. Repeat from * around. Sl st in 1st sc made. **6th rnd:** Sl st across to 1 st following p, sl st in loop, ch 4, holding back on hook the last loop of each tr, make 3 tr in same loop, thread over and draw through all loops on hook (cluster made), ch 3, p, ch 5, p, ch 3, make a 4-tr cluster in same loop. In each loop around make cluster, ch 3, p, ch 5, p, ch 3 and a cluster. Join last cluster to tip of 1st cluster. Fasten off.

SECOND MOTIF . . . Work as for 1st motif to 5th rnd incl. **6th rnd:** Complete 1st cluster as before, ch 3, p, ch 2, sc in corresponding loop of 1st motif, ch 2, p, ch 3, cluster in same place as last cluster and complete rnd as for 1st motif, joining next loop to adjacent loop of 1st motif as before. Make 5 x 11 motifs, joining motifs as 2nd was joined to 1st, leaving one free loop between joinings.

FILL-IN-LACE . . . Starting at center, ch 10. Join. **1st rnd:** 16 sc in ring. Join. **2nd rnd:** Ch 2, p, ch 2, sl st in free loop between joinings, ch 2, p, ch 2, skip 3 sc in ring, sc in next sc, ch 10, sl st in joining, ch 10, sc in same place as last sc. Repeat from beginning of rnd. Join and fasten off. Work Fill-in-lace in this manner in all sps between joinings.

EDGING . . . 1st rnd: Attach thread to a joining along outer edge, * ch 12, sc between p's of next loop. Repeat from * to within next joining, ch 12, sc in joining, ch 12, sc in next loop and continue thus around, ending with sl st in same place as thread was attached. **2nd rnd:** In each loop around, make 2 sc, 2 h dc, 2 dc, 9 tr, 2 dc, 2 h dc and 2 sc. Join with sl st to 1st sc made. Fasten off.

Pin runner to given measurements. Pat starch over Fill-in-laces with sponge or piece of cloth and press under a damp cloth. Be careful not to flatten rosettes.

DAISY CHAIN

Pretties for entertaining! Adorable crocheted daisies wreathe
around the dainty linen circles of this imported refreshment set.

MATERIALS: For best results use—

CLARK'S O.N.T. OR J. & P. COATS
BEST SIX CORD MERCERIZED CROCHET:

SMALL BALL:

CLARK'S O.N.T. OR J. & P. COATS, Size 50—*2 balls
each of 2 contrasting colors, to be referred to as
A and B.*

CLARK'S O.N.T. OR J. & P. COATS, Size 10—*1 ball of
Ecru.*

MILWARD'S *steel crochet hook No. 12 or 13.*

½ yd. linen 18 inches wide, to match color A or B.

Each small doily measures about 5⅛ inches in diameter; large doily measures about 14 inches in diameter.

SMALL DOILIES *(Make 6)... Motif...1st rnd:* To make
a ring, wind Ecru once around forefinger of left hand,
letting 6 inches of end hang free toward you. Insert hook through the ring on finger, place color A
across hook, and draw loop through; thread over and
draw through loop; slip Ecru loop off finger; then with
color A make 24 s c in ring, working over the double
thread. Drop color A and pull the Ecru ends of ring
tightly together. Tie ends and cut away only short end
of Ecru. Pick up color A, sl st in 1st s c made. **2nd
rnd:** With color A, working over Ecru ball thread,
make 9 s c. Ch 1, turn. * Make s c in each of 9 s c,
picking up the back loop only of each s c and working over the Ecru thread in order to conceal it; skip
1 s c of ring, s c in next s c, picking up both loops
and concealing Ecru as before (one petal made). Ch 1,
turn; s c in each of 4 s c on last petal, picking up
front loop only of each s c and working over Ecru
thread; then make 5 s c over Ecru thread (9 s c in all).
Ch 1, turn. Repeat from * around until 12 petals in all
are made. Then skip 1 s c of ring, s c in next s c, ch 1,
turn. Cut off Ecru, and join the first and last petals by
slip stitching together 4 s c at bottom of both petals.
Fasten off. Make 4 more motifs same as this. Then
make 5 more motifs in color B.

Cut a piece of linen 3¾ inches in diameter. Place
the 10 motifs around this piece of linen, alternating
colors and having motifs adjacent to one another.
Thread a needle with an 18-inch length of color A and
make a very narrow scallop of satin stitch on linen,
around 5 petals of color A motifs, at the same time
sewing the petals to linen. Continue thus around, making satin stitch in color to correspond with motif. Cut
away excess linen at back of work.

LARGE DOILY... Make 15 motifs each of color A and
color B. Cut a piece of linen 12 inches in diameter,
and complete as for small doilies.

19

MOTIF DOILY

ROYAL SOCIETY SIX CORD CORDICHET, Size 50: 2 balls of White or Ecru.

Steel Crochet Hook No. 12.

Doily measures 10 inches from point to point.

GAUGE: Each medallion measures 1¾ inches from point to point.

FIRST MEDALLION . . . Starting at center, ch 10. Join. **1st rnd:** Ch 4, holding back on hook the last loop of each d tr make 3 d tr in ring, thread over and draw through all loops on hook, (ch 6, holding back on hook the last loop of each d tr make 4 d tr in ring, thread over and draw through all loops on hook—a 4 d tr cluster made) 11 times; ch 6, sl st in top st of ch-4. **2nd rnd:** * 4 sc in next sp, ch 6, 4 sc in next sp. Repeat from * around. Sl st in 1st sc. **3rd rnd:** Ch 6, * 5 sc in next ch-6 sp, ch 4—a picot made—5 sc in same sp, ch 4, dc between 4-sc groups, ch 4. Repeat from * around, ending with ch 4, sl st in 3rd st of ch-6. Break off.

SECOND MEDALLION . . . Same as First Medallion through the 2nd rnd. **3rd rnd:** Ch 6, 5 sc in next sp, ch 2, sl st in 1st p of First Medallion, ch 2, 5 sc in same sp on Second Medallion, ch 2, sl st in next sp on First Medallion, ch 2, dc between 4-sc groups on Second Medallion, ch 2, sl st in next sp on First Medallion, ch 2, 5 sc in next sp on Second Medallion, ch 2, sl st in next p of First Medallion, ch 2, complete 3rd rnd as for First Medallion. Make 35 more medallions like this, joining as Second Medallion was joined to First and following chart for joinings.

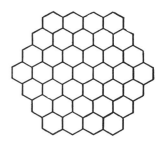

An Exquisite Full Blown Rose in Fine Filet

Capture summer's rose in pristine filet...a pattern always in demand with crocheters.

There are 10 spaces between heavy lines

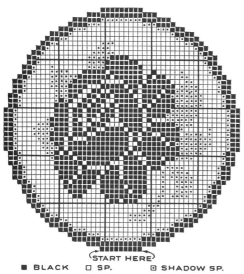

◼ BLACK ◻ SP. ▣ SHADOW SP.

Rose o' Summer

MATERIALS:

CLARK'S O.N.T. or J. & P. COATS BEST SIX CORD MERCERIZED CROCHET, size 50:

CLARK'S O.N.T.—2 balls of White or Ecru, or 3 balls of any color,

OR

J. & P. COATS —2 balls of White or Ecru.

Steel crochet hook No. 12.

Completed doily measures about 11½ inches in diameter.

GAUGE: 9 sps make 2 inches; 9 rows make 2 inches.

Starting at bottom of chart, ch 40. **1st row:** Tr in 5th ch from hook and in each ch across (37 tr counting 1st ch-4 as 1 tr). Ch 15, turn. **2nd row:** Tr in 5th ch from hook, tr in 10 ch (3 bls increased), tr in 36 tr, then make a foundation tr as follows: *Thread over hook twice, insert hook in top st of turning ch and draw loop through; thread over and draw through 1 loop (1 ch st made, to be used as a foundation st for next tr); complete tr in usual way.* Make 11 more foundation tr and 1 tr in the usual way (3 bls increased). Ch 15, turn. **3rd row:** Tr in 5th ch from hook, tr in 10 ch (3 bls increased), tr in 13 tr (3 bls over 3 bls), ch 1, skip 1 tr, tr in next tr, ch 1, skip 1 tr, tr in next tr (shadow sp over bl), make 8 more shadow sps, tr in 11 tr, foundation tr in top st of turning ch, make 11 more foundation tr and 1 tr in usual way (3 bls increased). Ch 7, turn. **4th row:** Tr in 5th ch from hook, tr in 2 tr, 3 bls, 3 shadow sps, ch 3, skip 3 tr, tr in next tr (sp over shadow sp), make 8 more sps, 3 shadow sps, tr in 11 tr, foundation tr in top st of turning ch, make 3 more foundation tr and 1 tr in usual way. Ch 11, turn.

5th and 6th rows: Follow chart. Ch 7 at end of 6th row. **7th row:** Tr in 5th ch from hook, tr in 2 tr, 2 bls, 2 shadow sps, 6 sps, ch 1, skip 1 ch, tr in next ch, ch 1, skip 1 ch, tr in next ch (shadow sp made over sp), make 3 more shadow sps, 13 sps, 2 shadow sps, 3 bls. Now follow chart until 10th row is complete. Ch 7 at end of 10th row. **11th row:** Tr in 5th ch from hook, tr in 2 tr, 1 bl, 1 shadow sp, 9 sps, 1 shadow sp, 4 sps, 3 tr in next tr (bl over sp), 2 bls, 1 sp, 2 bls, follow chart across row. Hereafter follow chart until 30th row is completed. Do not ch to turn. **31st row:** Sl st in 4 tr (1 sp decreased), ch 4, tr in 8 tr, 1 shadow sp, 4 sps, 6 shadow sps, 5 bls, 1 sp, 1 bl, 1 sp, 4 bls, 1 sp, 1 bl, 2 sps, 2 bls, 1 sp, 2 bls, 2 sps, 3 bls, 7 sps, 1 shadow sp, 2 bls. Ch 4, turn (1 bl decreased). Starting with 32nd row follow chart to top. Fasten off. Starch lightly and press.

Rose Hot Plate Mat Cover

MATERIALS REQUIRED: American Thread Company "DE LUXE" Mercerized Crochet and Knitting Cotton, Article 346 or "PURITAN" Bedspread Cotton, Article 40.

1 Ball of White
1 Ball of Green
1 Ball of Shaded Pinks or any Color desired.
Steel Crochet Hook No. 7.
1 8½ inch Round Hot Plate Mat.

With Shaded Pinks ch 7, join to form a ring, ch 7, d c into ring, * ch 3, d c into ring, repeat from * 5 times, ch 3, join in 3 rd st of ch 7.

2nd Row—Ch 1 and over each loop work 1 s c, 1 d c, 3 tr c, 1 d c, 1 s c, join.

3rd Row—Sl st in back of petal, * ch 5, s c between next 2 petals in back of work, repeat from * 7 times.

4th Row—Ch 1 and over each loop work 1 s c, 1 d c, 5 tr c, 1 d c, 1 s c, join.

5th Row—Slip st in back of petal, * ch 7, s c between next 2 petals in back of work, repeat from * 7 times, break thread.

6th Row—Attach Green, ch 1 and over each loop work 1 s c, 1 d c, 7 tr c, 1 d c, 1 s c, join, break thread.

7th Row—Attach White in 2nd tr c of Green petal, ch 7, skip 3 tr c, s c in next tr c, * ch 5, tr c between petals, ch 5, s c in 2nd tr c of next petal, ch 7, skip 3 tr c, s c in next tr c, repeat from * 6 times, ch 5, tr c between petals, ch 5, join.

8th Row—Sl st to loop, ch 3, d c in same space, ch 3, 2 d c in same space, 2 d c in next loop, ch 3, 2 d c in same loop (shell), work a shell in each loop, join in 3rd st of ch 3.

9th Row—Sl st to center of shell, ch 3, d c in same space, ch 3, 2 d c in same space, ch 1 and work a shell in center of each shell with ch 1 between shells, join.

10th Row—Sl st to center of shell, * ch 8, s c in center of next shell, repeat from * all around, break thread.

11th Row—Attach Shaded Pinks in loop, ch 3, 5 d c, ch 3, 6 d c in same loop, * 6 d c, ch 3, 6 d c in next loop, repeat from * all around, join.

12th Row—Ch 3 and work 1 d c in each d c and 2 d c, ch 3, 2 d c in each ch 3 loop, join.

13th Row—Ch 4 and work 1 tr c in each d c and 2 tr c, ch 3, 2 tr c in each ch 3 loop, join, break thread.

14th Row—Attach White in ch 3 loop at point, ch 3 and work a shell in same space, * ch 3, work a shell in next ch 3 loop, repeat from * all around, ch 3, join.

15th Row—Sl st to center of shell, ch 3 and work a shell in same space, * ch 4, shell in next shell, repeat from * all around, ch 4, join. Work 1 more row of shells with ch 5 between shells, break thread.

17th Row—Attach Shaded Pinks in shell, ch 3, 2 d c in same space, ch 3, 3 d c in same space, * ch 3, s c in next loop, ch 3, 3 d c, ch 3, 3 d c in next shell, repeat from * all around ending row with ch 3, s c in next loop, ch 3, join.

18th Row—Sl st to center of shell, ch 3, 2 d c in same space, * ch 3, s c in next s c, ch 3, 3 d c, ch 3, 3 d c in center of next shell, repeat from * all around ending row with ch 3, s c in next s c, ch 3, join, break thread.

19th Row—Start casing for Mat Cover. With wrong side of work toward you, join Shaded Pinks in loop of 16th row, * ch 10, s c over next loop of same row, repeat from * all around.

20th and 21st Rows—Sl st to center of loop and work a row of ch 9 loops, break thread.

FIELD OF DAISIES

MATERIALS: J. & P. COATS OR CLARK'S O.N.T. BEST SIX CORD MERCERIZED CROCHET, *Size 30:* **Small Ball:** J. & P. COATS—*12 balls of White or Ecru, or 16 balls of any color or* CLARK'S O.N.T.—*18 balls of White or Ecru, or 20 balls of any color . . . Steel Crochet Hook No. 10.*

GAUGE: Each motif measures 2 inches square.

FIRST MOTIF . . . Starting at center, ch 6. Join with sl st to form ring. **1st rnd:** 8 sc in ring. Join. **2nd rnd:** Ch 1, 2 sc in each sc around. Join. **3rd rnd:** Ch 1, sc in each sc around. Join. **4th rnd:** Ch 4, 4 tr in same place as sl st, * ch 2, skip 1 sc, 5 tr in next sc. Repeat from * around, ending with ch 2, sl st in top of ch-4. **5th rnd:** Ch 4, holding back on hook the last loop of each tr make tr in next 4 tr, thread over and draw through all loops on hook (cluster made); * ch 16, make a cluster over next 5 tr, ch 10, cluster over next 5 tr. Repeat from * around. Join and break off.

SECOND MOTIF . . . Work as for First Motif until 4th rnd is completed. **5th rnd:** Ch 4, make a cluster over next 4 tr, ch 8, sl st in corresponding loop on First Motif, ch 8, cluster over next 5 tr on Second Motif, ch 5, sl st in next loop on First Motif, ch 5, cluster over next 5 tr on Second Motif, ch 8, sl st in next loop on First Motif, ch 8, cluster over next 5 tr on Second Motif. Complete rnd as for First Motif.

Make 7 rows of 20 motifs, joining them as Second Motif was joined to First Motif (where 4 corners meet, join 3rd and 4th corners to joining of previous 2 corners).

EDGING . . . Attach thread to first sp following any corner loop and in each sp make (4 sc, ch 4) 3 times and 4 sc, having (4 sc, ch 4) 6 times and 4 sc in each corner loop. Join and break off.

Starch lightly and press.

A sprinkling of flowers on a table—a sparkle of color on a white cloth ... the newest and most charming idea in table decoration.

Pansy Doily Luncheon Set

MATERIALS: J. & P. Coats Tatting-Crochet, *Size 70: 4 balls of Bright Nile Green; 2 balls each of Shaded Fuchsia, Shaded Yellow, and Shaded Lavender; 1 ball of White . . . Steel Crochet Hooks No. 10 and No. 13.*

Large Doily measures 12 inches in diameter; Medium Doily 9 inches in diameter; Small Doily 6 inches in diameter

LARGE DOILY . . . Starting at center with Green and No. 13 hook, ch 10, join with sl st to form ring. **1st rnd:** 16 sc in ring, sl st in first sc made. **2nd rnd:** Sc in same place as sl st, * ch 5, skip 1 sc, sc in next sc. Repeat from * around, ending with ch 5. **3rd rnd:** * Sc in next sc, 2 sc in ch-5 sp, ch 5. Repeat from * around. **4th to 17th rnds incl:** * Skip first sc, sc in each remaining sc of sc group, 2 sc in ch-5 sp, ch 5. Repeat from * around; on 17th rnd end with the 17 sc of last group. **18th rnd:** Ch 5, * skip 1 sc, sc in next 15 sc, ch 5, sc in ch-5 sp, ch 5. Repeat from * around. **19th rnd:** * Skip 1 sc, sc in next 13 sc; (ch 5, sc in next loop) twice; ch 5. Repeat from * around. Continue in this manner, having 2 sc less in each sc group and 1 loop more between sc groups on each rnd until 1 sc remains in each sc group, and ending with ch 5, sc in loop preceding first sc.

Now work as follows: **26th to 30th rnds incl:** * Ch 6, sc in next loop. Repeat from * around (72 loops). **31st rnd:** Ch 7, sc in next loop, ch 7, sc in same loop (1 loop increased), inc 8 more loops evenly around (81 loops). **32nd to 40th rnds incl:** * Ch 7, sc in next loop. Repeat from * around. Join and break off at end of 40th rnd.

FIRST PANSY . . . Starting at center with Shaded Lavender and No. 10 hook, ch 6. Join with sl st to form ring. **1st rnd:** Ch 3, 2 dc in ring, (ch 7, 3 dc in ring) 4 times; ch 7. Join with sl st to top of ch-3. **2nd rnd:** Ch 3, (skip 1 dc, dc in next dc, 15 tr in next sp, dc in next dc) 3 times; * skip 1 dc, dc in next dc, ch 1, in next sp make (tr, ch 1) twice; (d tr, ch 1) 3 times; (tr tr, ch 1) 5 times; (d tr, ch 1) 3 times and (tr, ch 1) twice; dc in next dc, ch 1. Repeat from * until another large petal is

completed. Join and break off. Make 8 more Lavender Pansies, 9 Yellow and 9 Fuchsia.

To Join Pansies: Attach White to center tr of center small petal on Lavender Pansy, sc in same place, sl st in any loop on doily, ch 3, sl st in next loop, ch 1, skip 1 tr on next small petal, tr in next tr, ch 3, sl st in next loop on doily, ch 1, tr in next-to-last tr on first small petal of next Yellow pansy, ch 3, sl st in next loop on doily, sl st in center tr of next petal on pansy. Complete joining as before. Join a Fuchsia pansy the same way. Join remaining pansies, alternating colors as before. Join and break off White.

EDGING . . . Attach White to first ch-1 sp on first large petal of any pansy, ch 4, * dc in next sp, ch 1. Repeat from * across 2 large petals. Ch 3, dc in next ch-1 sp on next large petal, ch 1 and work in this manner all around. Join and break off.

MEDIUM DOILY . . . Work as for Large Doily until 30 rnds are completed. Join and break off (72 loops).

PANSIES . . . Make 6 pansies of each color.

To Join Pansies: Attach White to center tr of 2nd small petal on Lavender Pansy, sc in same tr, sl st in any loop on doily, ch 3, sl st in next loop, ch 1, skip 1 tr on next petal, tr in next tr, (ch 3, sl st in next loop on doily) twice; ch 3, tr in next-to-last tr on first small petal on next Yellow Pansy. Join as before, having 1 extra loop between each pansy around. Complete as for Large Doily.

SMALL DOILY . . . Work as for Large Doily until 10 rnds are completed. **11th rnd:** Ch 5, * skip 1 sc, sc in next 8 sc, ch 5, sc in next ch-5 sp, ch 5. Repeat from * around. **12th, 13th and 14th rnds:** Work as before, having 2 sc less and 1 loop more between sc groups. **15th rnd:** * Skip 1 sc, sc in next sc, (ch 5, sc in next loop) 5 times; ch 5. Repeat from * around. **16th rnd:** * Ch 5, sc in next loop. Repeat from * around. Join and break off (48 loops). Make 4 pansies of each color. Join as for Medium Doily.

Alternate wedges of picture...pretty filet and horizontal strips for a smart viewpoint.

Two-in-One

MATERIALS:

CLARK'S O.N.T. or J. & P. COATS BEST SIX CORD MERCERIZED CROCHET, size 20:

SMALL BALL:
CLARK'S O.N.T.—3 balls of White or Ecru,
OR
J. & P. COATS —2 balls of White or Ecru.

BIG BALL:
J. & P. COATS —1 ball of White or Ecru.

Steel crochet hook No. 9 or 10.

Completed doily measures about 12 inches across.

GAUGE: 4½ sps make 1 inch; 4½ rows make 1 inch.

Starting at bottom of chart, ch 66. **1st row:** Dc in 4th ch from hook and in each ch across (64 dc, counting 1st ch-3 as 1 dc). Ch 5, turn. **2nd row:** Dc in 4th ch from hook, dc in next ch, dc in next dc (1 bl increased), ch 2, skip 2 dc, dc in next dc (sp over bl), make 19 more sps, ch 2, skip 2 dc, then make a foundation dc as follows: *Thread over, insert hook in top st of turning ch and draw a loop through; thread over and draw through 1 loop (1 ch st made, to be used as a foundation st for next dc); complete dc in usual way.* Make 2 more foundation

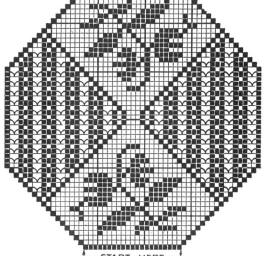

There are 10 spaces between heavy lines

← START HERE →

dc and 1 dc in usual way (1 bl increased). Ch 5, turn. **3rd row:** Follow chart across. **4th row:** 1 bl, 5 sps, 2 dc in next sp, dc in next dc (bl over sp), 7 sps, 1 bl, 11 sps, 1 bl. Ch 5, turn. Now follow chart until 12th row is completed. Ch 5, turn. **13th row:** 1 bl, ch 3, skip 2 dc, sc in next dc, ch 3, skip 2 ch, dc in next dc (lacet), 2 bls, 1 sp, 1 bl, 7 sps, 5 bls, 5 sps, 1 bl, 1 sp, 7 bls, 5 sps, 1 bl, 1 sp, 2 bls, ch 3, skip 2 ch, sc in next dc, ch 3, skip 2 dc, foundation dc in top st of turning ch (lacet), 1 bl. Ch 5, turn.

14th row: 1 bl, 1 sp, ch 5, dc in next dc (bar over lacet), (1 bl, 1 sp) twice; 1 bl, 7 sps, 3 bls, 1 bl, 1 bl, 3 sps, 2 bls, 2 sps, 5 bls, 5 sps, (1 bl, 1 sp) twice; 1 bl, ch 5, dc in next dc (bar over lacet),

1 sp, 1 bl. Ch 5, turn. **15th row:** 1 bl, 1 sp, 1 bl, ch 3, sc in bar, ch 3, dc in next dc (lacet over bar), 3 bls, lacet, 1 bl, 3 sps, 4 bls, 3 sps, 4 bls, 2 sps, 1 bl, 1 sp, 6 bls, 3 sps, 1 bl, lacet, lacet, 1 bl, 1 sp, 1 bl. Ch 5, turn. Starting with 16th row follow chart until the 38th row is completed. Do not ch to turn. **39th row:** Sl st across 1st bl (1 bl decreased), ch 3, 3 dc in bar, ch 2, dc in next dc, (3 bls, lacet) twice; 1 bl, 1 sp, 1 bl, 8 sps, 1 bl, 1 sp, 6 bls, 7 sps, 1 bl, 1 sp, 1 bl, (lacet, 3 bls) twice; 1 sp, 1 bl (another bl decreased). Turn. Starting with 40th row follow chart to top. Fasten off.

There are 10 spaces
between heavy lines

START HERE

Midsummer Day

MATERIALS:

CLARK'S O.N.T. or J. & P. COATS BEST SIX CORD MERCERIZED CROCHET, size 50:

CLARK'S O.N.T.—6 balls of White or Ecru, or 7 balls of any color,
OR
J. & P. COATS —4 balls of White or Ecru.
Steel crochet hook No. 11 or 12.
Completed doily measures about 15 x 21 inches.

GAUGE: 6 sps make 1 inch; 6 rows make 1 inch.

Starting at bottom of chart, ch 68. **1st row:** Dc in 8th ch from hook, (ch 2, skip 2 ch, dc in next ch) 20 times. Ch 13, turn. **2nd row:** Dc in 8th ch from hook, ch 2, skip 2 ch, dc in next ch, ch 2, dc in next dc (3 sps increased); 2 dc in next sp, dc in next dc (bl over sp), make 20 more bls, ch 5, dc in same place as last dc (1 sp increased); (ch 5, dc in 3rd st of last ch-5) twice (2 more sps increased); turn, sl st in 1st 3 ch. Ch 7, do not turn. **3rd row:** Dc in same place as last sl st (1 sp increased), 10 bls, ch 2, skip 2 dc, dc in next dc (sp over bl), make 1 more sp, 3 bls, 2 sps, 10 bls, ch 5, dc in same place as last dc, turn, sl st in 1st 3 ch (1 sp increased). Ch 10, turn. **4th row:** Dc in 8th ch from hook, ch 2, dc in next dc, 2 bls, 6 sps, 1 bl, 5 sps, 1 bl, 5 sps, 1 bl, 6 sps, 2 bls, ch 5, dc in same place as last dc, ch 5, dc in 3rd st of last ch-5. Ch 7, turn. Starting at 5th row, follow chart to top. This completes one half of doily. Omit last row on chart and work back until 26 more rows are complete. Do not ch to turn at end of last row. Sl st in each ch and in next dc. Ch 5 and follow chart across to within 1 sp from end of row (1 sp decreased at both ends). Now follow chart back to 1st row to complete doily. Do not break off but work a row of sc closely around edges keeping work flat. Join and fasten off.

Apple Blossom Place Mat

MATERIALS: J. & P. Coats Tatting-Crochet, *Size 70, 1 ball of Shaded Pink and 1 ball of Shaded Yellow. Scraps of Dark Brown Pearl Cotton . . . Steel Crochet Hooks No. 10 and No. 14 . . . J. & P. Coats or Clark's O.N.T. Six Strand Embroidery Floss, 1 skein of Colonial Brown . . . A piece of pink organdy, 12 x 18 inches.*

APPLE BLOSSOM (Make 12) . . .
Starting at center with Pink and No. 14 hook, ch 10. Join with sl st to form ring. **1st rnd:** Ch 1, 25 sc in ring. Join.

Now work petals individually as follows.

FIRST PETAL . . . 1st row: 2 sc in next 5 sc. Ch 1, turn. **2nd to 7th rows incl:** Sc in each sc across. Ch 1, turn. Do not turn at end of 7th row.

SECOND PETAL . . . Sl st in end sc of each row. **Next row:** 2 sc in next 5 sc on center. Ch 1, turn. Work as for First Petal. Complete other petals to correspond.

Make a narrow hem around outer edge of organdy. Using 3 strands of Embroidery Floss, embroider blanket stitch around outer edge of Mat. Embroider a French knot between each bar of blanket stitch.

STEM . . . Using Brown Pearl Cotton double and No. 10 hook make a chain 6 inches long, make 6 lengths of chain, each 3 inches long, and 5 lengths, each 4 inches long.

Sew these chains to Mat, to form a branch as shown in illustration. Sew an Apple Blossom to end of each stem.

With Yellow make a chain 2 inches long, sew to center of Apple Blossom, making 5 loops (for stamens). Complete all flowers in this manner. Starch lightly and press.

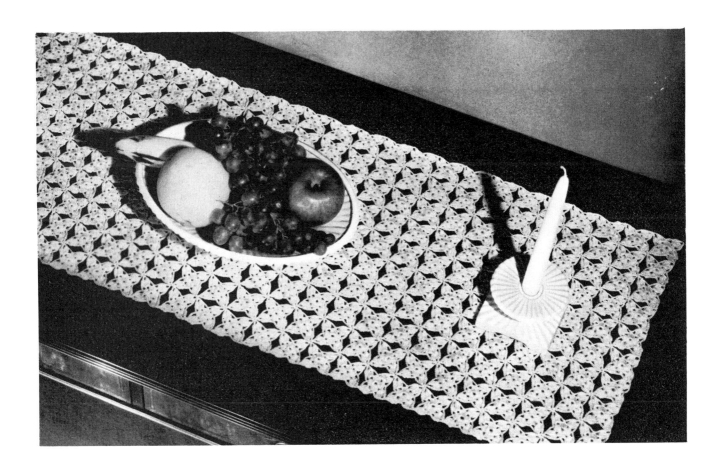

BUTTERCUP

MATERIALS: CLARK'S O.N.T. OR J. & P. COATS
PEARL COTTON, *size 5, 16 balls.*
MILWARD'S *steel crochet hook No. 7.*
Completed runner measures about 15″ x 45″.
GAUGE: Motif measures 1½ inches across sides.

MOTIF ... Ch 5, join with sl st. **1st rnd:** Ch 3 (to count as d c), 2 d c in ring; * ch 3 (corner), 5 d c in ring. Repeat from * twice, ch 3, 2 d c in ring, sl st in top of 1st ch-3. **2nd rnd:** Ch 5, * make 3 tr in corner ch-3, retaining on hook last loop of each tr; thread over and draw through all loops on hook, ch 1 tightly (cluster); ch 3 for corner, make another cluster in same sp, ch 4, s c in center d c of 5-d c group, ch 4. Repeat from *, joining last ch-4 to 1st ch of 1st ch-5. Fasten off. This completes first motif.

SECOND MOTIF...Work 1st rnd as for previous motif. **2nd rnd:** Ch 5, cluster in corner ch-3, ch 1, drop loop from hook and insert hook in corresponding sp between 2 clusters of previous motif, draw loop through; ch 2, another cluster in same sp on motif in work, ch 4, s c in center d c of 5-d c group, ch 4, cluster in next corner, ch 1, join as before to corresponding corner of previous motif (ch 2, after joining); cluster in same sp on motif in work. Complete rnd as for previous motif (no more joinings).

Work 10 x 29 motifs, joining at all corresponding corners.

Daisy Luncheon Set

MATERIALS: J. & P. Coats or Clark's O.N.T. Best Six Cord Mercerized Crochet, *Size 50 (Small Ball), 4 balls of White . . . Steel Crochet Hook No. 12 . . . 1 yard of yellow linen.*

PLACE DOILY (Make 2)—Motifs (Make 106) . . . Starting at center, ch 7. Join with sl st to form ring. **1st rnd:** 24 sc in ring. Sl st in first sc. **2nd rnd:** Attach a new piece of thread and working over original thread make 9 sc over it. Ch 1, turn. * Make sc in next 9 sc, picking up the back loop only of each sc and working over original thread in order to conceal it, skip 1 sc on ring, sc in next sc concealing original thread as before (one petal made). Ch 1, turn. Sc in each of next 4 sc on last petal picking up front loop of each sc only and working over original thread; now make 5 sc over original thread (9 sc in all). Ch 1, turn. Repeat from * until 12 petals in all are made. Skip 1 sc on ring, sc in next sc. Ch 1, turn. Cut off original thread and join the first and last petals together by slip stitching together the last 4 sc at base of both petals. Break off.

Cut a piece of yellow linen, 12 inches in diameter. Starch motifs lightly and press. Pin 30 motifs in place along outer edges of linen. Work in blanket st along inner edge of motifs, thus forming scallops. Cut off excess linen.

BREAD AND BUTTER DOILY (Make 2) . . . Cut a piece of yellow linen, 6 inches in diameter. Pin 14 motifs in place along outer edges and finish as for Place Doily.

GLASS DOILY (Make 2) . . . Cut a piece of yellow linen, 4 inches in diameter. Pin 9 motifs in place along outer edges and finish as for Place Doily.

Blue Bell Doily

MATERIALS: J. & P. COATS OR CLARK'S O.N.T. BEST SIX CORD MERCERIZED CROCHET, *Size 30:* **Small Ball:** J. & P. COATS—*3 balls of White,* or CLARK'S O.N.T.—*5 balls of White* . . . J. & P. COATS TATTING-CROCHET, *Size 70, 2 balls of Blue . . . Scraps of Green Pearl Cotton . . . Yellow Stamens . . . Steel Crochet Hooks No. 10 and No. 14.*

Doily measures 15 inches in diameter

Starting at center with White and No. 10 hook, ch 10. Join with sl st to form ring. **1st rnd:** Ch 3, 25 dc in ring. Join to top of ch-3. **2nd rnd:** Sc in same place as sl st, * ch 5, skip 1 dc, sc in next dc. Repeat from * around, ending with ch 2, dc in first sc. **3rd rnd:** * Ch 6, sc in next loop. Repeat from * around, ending with ch 3, dc in dc. **4th rnd:** * Ch 7, sc in next loop. Repeat from * around, ending with ch 3, tr in dc. **5th rnd:** * Ch 9, sc in 5th ch from hook (picot made); ch 4, sc in next loop. Repeat from * around, ending with ch 4, sl st in tr. Ch 5, turn. **6th rnd:** Sl st in last tr made, turn, sl st in ch-5 loop, ch 4, in same loop make 2 tr, ch 3 and 3 tr; * ch 5, in next picot make 3 tr, ch 3 and 3 tr (shell made). Repeat from * around, ending with ch 3, sl st in 4th ch of ch-4. **7th rnd:** Sl st to sp of next shell, ch 4, in same sp make 2 tr, ch 3 and 3 tr (shell made over shell); * ch 7, shell in sp of next shell. Repeat from * around. Join. **8th, 9th**

and **10th rnds:** Same as last rnd, having 1 ch more between shells on each rnd. **11th rnd:** Same as last rnd, having 12 ch between shells. **12th rnd:** * Shell over shell, ch 7, sc in next sp, ch 7. Repeat from * around. Join. **13th rnd:** * Shell over shell, ch 7, tr in next sc, ch 7. Repeat from * around. Join. **14th rnd:** Sl st to sp of next shell, ch 4, in same sp make 2 tr, ch 5 and 3 tr; * ch 9, sc in next tr, ch 9, in sp of next shell make 3 tr, ch 5 and 3 tr. Repeat from * around. Join. **15th rnd:** Sl st to sp of next shell, ch 5, 12 d tr in same sp, * ch 15, 13 d tr in sp of next shell. Repeat from * around. Join. **16th rnd:** Ch 6, (d tr in next d tr, ch 1) 11 times; * d tr in next d tr, ch 6, sc in next sp, ch 6, (d tr in next d tr, ch 1) 12 times. Repeat from * around. Join. **17th rnd:** Ch 7, (d tr in next d tr, ch 2) 11 times; * d tr in next d tr, ch 5, (d tr in next d tr, ch 2) 12 times. Repeat from * around. Join.

Now complete scallops individually as follows:

FIRST SCALLOP . . . 1st row: (In next sp make sc, ch 1, dc, ch 1 and sc) 12 times. Ch 8, turn. **2nd row:** (D tr between next 2 sc, ch 3) 11 times; d tr in next sc. Turn. **3rd row:** In each sp across make sc, ch 1, 3 dc, ch 1, and sc (shell made); ch 5, sl st in top of first d tr on next scallop.

SECOND SCALLOP . . . 1st row: Repeat first row of First Scallop. **2nd**

row: (D tr between next 2 sc, ch 3) 11 times; sl st in top of next ch. Turn. **3rd row:** Repeat 3rd row of First Scallop. Complete other Scallops to correspond. Join last shell of last scallop to first shell made.

Next rnd: Sl st to center dc of 2nd shell on First Scallop, sc in same place, * ch 20, skip 2 shells, sc in center dc of next shell. Repeat from * around. Join. **Following rnd:** Sl st to center of next loop, ch 3, holding back on hook the last loop of each dc, make 3 dc in same loop, thread over and draw through all loops on hook (cluster made); * ch 18, make a 4-dc cluster in next loop. Repeat from * around. Join and break off.

BLUE BELL (Make 13) . . . Starting at center with Blue and No. 14 hook, ch 5. Join with sl st to form ring. **1st rnd:** Ch 4, 14 tr in ring. Join. **2nd rnd:** Ch 4, tr in same place as sl st, 2 tr in next tr, * tr in next tr, 2 tr in next 2 tr. Repeat from * around, ending with tr in last tr. Join. **3rd rnd:** Sc in same place as sl st, sc in each tr around (25 sc). Join. **4th rnd:** Ch 4, tr in same sc as sl st, 2 tr in each sc around. Join.

FIRST PETAL . . . 1st row: Ch 4, holding back on hook the last loop of each tr make tr in next 2 tr, thread over and draw through all loops on hook (cluster made); tr in next 3 tr, cluster over next 3 tr. Ch 4, turn. **2nd row:** Holding back on hook the last loop of each tr make 2 tr in tip of next cluster, tr in next 3 tr, 2 tr in tip of next cluster, thread over and complete a cluster; ch 4, turn, sl st at base of cluster, ch 4, sl st in next 2 tr on Blue Bell, ch 4, and work next petal as for First Petal until 5 petals are completed. Join and break off.

LEAF AND STEM (Make 13) . . . Using Green and No. 10 hook, ch 17, sc in 2nd ch from hook and in next 6 ch, (ch 7, sc in 2nd ch from hook and in next 6 ch, sl st in same ch as last sc on starting chain) twice; ch 9. Break off.

Sew stems around doily. Sew stamens to flowers. Apply sizing to flowers to preserve shape. Sew flowers in place.

Pink Clover Doily

MATERIALS: J. & P. Coats or Clark's O.N.T. Best Six Cord Mercerized Crochet, *Size 30:* **Small Ball:** J. & P. Coats—*2 balls of White or Ecru, or* Clark's O.N.T.—*3 balls of White or Ecru* . . . Clark's O.N.T. "Brilliant" — *2 balls of Hunter's Green* . . . J. & P. Coats or Clark's O.N.T. Six Strand Embroidery Floss, *1 skein of Shaded Rose* . . . Steel Crochet Hook No. 10.

Doily measures 14 inches in diameter

Starting at center ch 6. Join with sl st to form ring. **1st rnd:** 8 sc in ring. **2nd rnd:** 2 sc in each sc around. **3rd rnd:** Sc in each sc around. **4th rnd:** * Ch 20, skip 1 sc, sc in next sc. Repeat from * around. Join and break off. **5th rnd:** Attach thread to any loop, ch 4, 3 tr in same loop, ch 4, sc in top of last tr made (picot), 3 tr in same loop, * ch 8, make 4 tr, picot and 3 tr in next loop. Repeat from * around, ending with ch 3, d tr in top of starting chain. **6th rnd:** Ch 4, 3 tr in same sp, picot, 3 tr in same sp, * ch 11, in next sp make 4 tr, picot and 3 tr. Repeat from * around. Join. **7th rnd:** Sl st in next 3 tr and in next picot, ch 4, 7 tr in same picot, * ch 9, sc in next sp, ch 9, 8 tr in next picot loop. Repeat from * around. Join. **8th rnd:** Ch 4, tr in next 2 tr, * ch 4, sl st in next 2 tr, ch 4, tr in next 3 tr, ch 4, sc in next loop, ch 8, sc in next loop, ch 4, tr in next 3 tr. Repeat from * around. Join. **9th rnd:** Ch 4, tr in next 2 tr, * tr in top of next ch, ch 15, tr in top of next ch, tr in next 3 tr, ch 5, skip next sp, sc in next loop, ch 5, tr in next 3 tr. Repeat from * around. Join. **10th rnd:** Ch 4, tr in next 3 tr, * 18 tr in next sp, tr in next 4 tr, ch 5, tr in next 4 tr. Repeat from * around. Join. **11th rnd:** Ch 4, tr in next 3 tr, * (ch 10, skip 7 tr, tr in next 4 tr) twice; tr in next 4 tr. Repeat from * around. Join. **12th rnd:** Ch 4, tr in next 3 tr, * ch 2, skip 1 ch, tr in next ch, (ch 1, skip 1 ch, tr in next ch) 4 times; ch 1, skip 1 tr, (tr in next tr, ch 1) twice; tr in next ch, (ch 1, skip 1 ch, tr in next ch) 4 times; ch 2, tr in

next 8 tr. Repeat from * around. Join. **13th rnd:** Ch 6, tr tr in next 3 tr, * ch 9, skip 4 tr, sl st in next tr, across next 3 sps and following tr, ch 9, skip 4 tr, tr tr in next 4 tr, ch 6, tr tr in next 4 tr. Repeat from * around. Join. **14th rnd:** Ch 4, tr in next 3 tr tr, * (ch 1, skip 1 st, tr in next st) 12 times; ch 1, tr in next 4 tr tr, 12 tr in next sp, tr in next 4 tr tr. Repeat from * around. Join. **15th rnd:** Ch 4, tr in next 3 tr, * ch 7, skip 5 sps, tr in next sp, tr in next 2 tr, tr in next sp, ch 7, skip 5 sps, tr in next 4 tr, ch 6, skip 4 tr, tr in next tr, ch 6, skip 2 tr, tr in next tr, ch 6, skip 4 tr, tr in next 4 tr. Repeat from * around. Join. **16th rnd:** Ch 4, tr in next 3 tr, * (tr in next 7 ch, tr in next 4 tr) twice; (ch 6, tr in next sp) 3 times; ch 6, tr in next 4 tr. Repeat from * around. Join. **17th rnd:** Ch 4, tr in next 2 tr, * ch 4, sl st in next 20 tr, ch 4, tr in next 3 tr, (ch 7, tr in next sp) 4 times; ch 7, tr in next 3 tr. Repeat from * around. Join. **18th rnd:** Ch 4, tr in next 2 tr, * tr in top of next 2 chains, tr in next 3 tr, (ch 7, tr in next sp) 5 times; ch 7, tr in next 3 tr.

(Continued on page 35.)

Black Eyed Susan Doily

MATERIALS: J. & P. Coats or Clark's O.N.T. Best Six Cord Mercerized Crochet, *Size 30, 2 balls (Small Balls) each of White and Dark Yellow* . . . J. & P. Coats or Clark's O.N.T. Pearl Cotton, *Size 5, 1 ball of Black* . . . Steel Crochet Hook No. 10.

Doily measures 12 inches in diameter

CENTER . . . Starting at center with Yellow, ch 10. Join with sl st to form ring. **1st rnd:** Ch 3, 23 dc in ring. Join with sl st to top of ch-3. **2nd rnd:** * Ch 4, tr in same place as sl st, tr in next dc, ch 4, sl st in same place as last tr, sl st in next dc. Repeat from * around. **3rd rnd:** Sl st in next 4 ch, ch 4, holding back on hook the last loop of each tr make tr in next 2 tr, tr in next ch, thread over and draw through all loops on hook (cluster made), * ch 10, holding back on hook the last loop of each tr make tr in top

of next ch-4, tr in next 2 tr, tr in next ch, thread over and draw through all loops on hook (another cluster made). Repeat from * around (12 petals). Join and break off. **4th rnd:** Attach White at tip of any cluster, in each sp around make 7 sc, ch 3 and 7 sc; sl st in first sc (12 points made). **5th rnd:** Sl st in next 7 sc and in next ch-3 loop, ch 4, in same loop make tr, ch 4 and 2 tr; * ch 7, in next ch-3 loop make 2 tr, ch 4 and 2 tr. Repeat from * around. Join with sl st to top of ch-4. **6th rnd:** Sl st in next tr and in next sp, ch 4, in same sp make tr, ch 4 and 2 tr; * ch 4, sc in next sp, ch 3, sc in same sp, ch 4, in next sp make 2 tr, ch 4 and 2 tr. Repeat from * around. Join. **7th rnd:** Sl st in next tr and in next sp, ch 4, in same sp make tr, ch 5 and 2 tr; * ch 6, skip next sp, sc in next loop, ch 6, skip next sp, in next sp between tr's make 2 tr, ch 5 and 2 tr. Repeat from * around. Join. **8th rnd:** Sl st in

next tr and in next sp, ch 4, make 10 tr in same sp, * ch 3, tr in each of next 2 sps, ch 3, 11 tr in next sp. Repeat from * around. Join. **9th rnd:** Ch 5, (tr in next tr, ch 1) 9 times; * tr in next tr, ch 5, sc in each of next 2 ch-3 sps; ch 5, (tr in next tr, ch 1) 10 times. Repeat from * around. Join to 4th ch of ch-5. **10th rnd:** Ch 6, * (tr in next tr, ch 2) 9 times; tr in next 2 tr, ch 2. Repeat from * around, ending with tr in last tr. Join to 4th ch of ch-6. **11th rnd:** Sl st in next sp, (ch 5, sc in next sp) 3 times; * ch 4, skip next tr, in next tr make tr, ch 5 and tr; ch 4, skip next sp, sc in next sp, (ch 5, sc in next ch-2 sp) 7 times. Repeat from * around. Join and break off.

FLOWER MOTIF (Make 12)—First Motif . . . With Yellow work as for Center until 3rd rnd is completed. **4th rnd:** Attach White at tip of any cluster, *(Continued on page 35.)*

Blue Aster Doily

MATERIALS: J. & P. Coats or Clark's O.N.T. Best Six Cord Mercerized Crochet, *Size 30:* **Small Ball:** J. & P. Coats—*3 balls of White,* or Clark's O.N.T.—*4 balls of White* . . . J. & P. Coats Tatting-Crochet, *Size 70, 2 balls of Blue* . . . J. & P. Coats or Clark's O.N.T. Pearl Cotton, *Size 5: 1 ball of Orange* . . . *Scraps of Blue* . . . *Steel Crochet Hooks No. 10 and No. 14.*

**Doily measures
12½ inches in diameter**

Starting at center with White and No. 10 hook, ch 10. Join with sl st to form ring. **1st rnd:** Ch 3, 27 dc in ring. Join. **2nd rnd:** Sc in same place as sl st, * ch 3, sc in next dc. Repeat from * around. Join. **3rd, 4th and 5th rnds:** Sl st to center of next loop, sc in same loop, * ch 3, sc in next loop. Repeat from * around. Join. **6th rnd:** Same as last rnd, making ch-4 loops instead of ch-3. **7th and 8th rnds:** Same as last rnd, making ch-5 loops instead of ch-4. **9th rnd:** Sl st to center of next loop, ch 6, tr tr in next loop, ch 6, sc in top of tr tr (picot made), * ch 11, holding back on hook the last loop of each tr tr make tr tr in next 2 loops, thread over and draw through all loops on hook (joint tr tr made); ch 6, sc in top of joint tr tr (another

picot made). Repeat from * around. Join. **10th rnd:** Sl st to center of next picot, ch 5, holding back on hook the last loop of each d tr make 4 d tr in same loop, thread over and draw through all loops on hook (cluster made); * ch 6, sc in tip of cluster, ch 12, make a 5-d tr cluster in next picot loop. Repeat from * around. Join.

11th rnd: Same as 10th rnd, making ch 15 (instead of ch-12) between clusters. **12th rnd:** Sl st in next picot, ch 6, (d tr in same loop, ch 1) 9 times; d tr in same loop, * ch 7, sc in next sp, ch 7, in next picot loop make (d tr, ch 1) 10 times and d tr. Repeat from * around. Join. **13th rnd:** Sl st in next

(Continued on page 35.)

34

Blue Aster

(Continued from page 34.)

sp, sc in same sp, * (ch 4, sc in next sp) 9 times; 7 sc in each of the next 2 sps, sc in next sp. Repeat from * around. Join. **14th rnd:** Sl st to center of next loop, sc in same loop, * (ch 4, sc in next loop) 8 times; ch 10, sc in next loop. Repeat from * around. Join. **15th rnd:** Sl st to center of next loop, sc in same loop, * (ch 4, sc in next loop) 6 times; ch 4, 2 sc in next loop, 11 sc in next sp, 2 sc in next loop. Repeat from * around, ending with 2 sc in first loop (over sl sts). Join. **16th rnd:** Sl st to center of next loop, sc in same loop, * (ch 4, sc in next loop) 6 times; ch 6, skip 7 sc, sc in next sc, ch 6, sc in next loop. Repeat from * around. Join. **17th rnd:** Sl st to center of next loop, sc in same loop, * (ch 4, sc in next loop) 4 times; ch 4, 2 sc in next loop, 6 sc in next sp, ch 1, 6 sc in next sp, 2 sc in next loop. Repeat from * around, ending with 2 sc in first loop (over sl sts). Join. **18th rnd:** Sl st to center of next loop, sc in same loop, * (ch 4, sc in next loop) 4 times; ch 6, tr in next ch-1 sp, ch 6, sc in next loop. Repeat from * around. Join. **19th rnd:** Sl st to center of next loop, sc in same loop, * (ch 4, sc in next loop) twice; ch 4, 2 sc in next loop, 6 sc in next sp, ch 1, 6 sc in next sp, 2 sc in next loop. Repeat from * around, ending with 2 sc in first loop (over sl st). Join. **20th rnd:** Sl st to center of next loop, sc in same loop, * (ch 4, sc in next loop) twice; ch 11, sc in next ch-1 sp, ch 11, sc in next loop. Repeat from * around. Join. **21st rnd:** Sl st to center of next loop, ch 4, tr in next loop, * (ch 12, sc in next loop) twice; ch 12, holding back on hook the last loop of each tr, make tr in next 2 loops, thread over and draw through all loops on hook (joint tr made). Repeat from * around, ending with ch 6, tr tr in top of starting chain. **22nd rnd:** Ch 3, 3 dc in top of tr tr, ch 3, sl st in same place, * ch 12, sc in next loop, ch 3, 3 dc in last sc made, ch 3, sl st in same place. Repeat from * around. Join and break off. Starch lightly and press.

ASTER (Make 7) . . . Starting at center with Blue Tatting-Crochet, and No. 14 hook, ch 10. Join with sl st to form ring. **1st rnd:** 24 sc in ring. Sl st in first sc. **2nd rnd:** * Ch 14, sc in 2nd ch from hook and in each ch across, sc in next 2 sc on ring (one petal completed). Repeat from * around (12 petals). **3rd rnd:** * Working over 2 strands of Light Blue Pearl Cotton, sc in each ch of next petal, 5 sc in last ch; working over the 2 strands as before and over the sc's of

petal make sc at base of each sc of petal, skip 1 sc on ring, sc in next sc. Repeat from * around. Sl st in first sc. Break off.

CENTER . . . Starting at center with Orange, ch 2. **1st rnd:** 5 sc in 2nd ch from hook. **2nd rnd:** 2 sc in back loop of each sc. **3rd rnd:** * Sc in back loop of next sc, 2 sc in back loop of next sc. Repeat from * around. **4th and 5th rnds:** Sc in back loop of each sc around. Sl st in next sc. Break off. Stuff center with cotton batting or scraps of thread and sew neatly in place. Sew Asters in place as in illustration.

Pink Clover

(Continued from page 32.)

Repeat from * around. Join. **19th rnd:** Ch 4, holding back on hook the last loop of each tr, make tr in next 7 tr, thread over and draw through all loops on hook (cluster made); * (ch 7, tr in next sp) 6 times; ch 7, cluster over next 8 tr. Repeat from * around, ending with ch 3, tr in tip of first cluster. **20th rnd:** Ch 4, * tr in next sp, (ch 10, sc in 5th ch from hook—picot made—ch 5, tr in next sp) 6 times. Repeat from * around. Join and break off.

FOUR LEAF CLOVER (Make 8) . . . Starting at center with Green, ch 10. Join with sl st to form ring.

First Leaf: 1st row: Sl st in ring, ch 4, tr in ring. Ch 3, turn. **2nd row:** 2 dc in first tr, 3 dc in next ch. Ch 1, turn. **3rd row:** 2 sc in first dc, sc in each dc across, 2 sc in top of next ch. Ch 3, turn. **4th row:** Holding back on hook the last loop of each dc, make dc in next 3 sc, thread over and draw through all loops on hook (cluster made), ch 3, sl st in next sc, ch 3, make another cluster, ch 3, sl st in last sc. Break off.

Second Leaf: Attach thread to ring, ch 4, and complete Leaf as before. Make 2 more leaves in this manner. Now work sc closely along outer edges of First Leaf to within first tr at base of leaf, work sc over this tr-bar, making sc's in corresponding sc on opposite side of leaf. Sl st in ring and work sc in this manner all around outer edges of all leaves. Do not break off.

STEM . . . Make a chain 6 inches long. Sc in 2nd ch from hook and in each ch across, sl st in ring. Break off.

BUD (Make 8) . . . Ch 5, tr in 5th ch from hook, ch 3, turn and complete as for Four Leaf Clover until first leaf is

completed. Sc around this piece as before. Break off.

FLOWER . . . **1st row:** Mark off 9 sc on top of Bud. Using 3 strands of Rose, attach thread to first sc, sc in same place, half dc in next sc, dc in next 2 sc, tr in next sc, dc in next 2 sc, half dc in next sc, sc in next sc. Ch 1, turn. **2nd row:** Sc in first sc, * ch 3, sc in next st. Repeat from * across. Break off.

Sew Leaves and Flowers in place as in illustration. Starch lightly and press.

Black Eyed Susan

(Continued from page 33.)

7 sc in next sp, ch 1, sl st in center ch-5 loop of any scallop on Center, ch 1, 7 sc in same sp on Motif, 7 sc in next sp on Motif, ch 1, skip 2 loops on center, sl st in next loop, ch 1, 7 sc in same sp on Motif, 7 sc in next sp on Motif, ch 1, skip 3 loops on Center, sl st in next loop, ch 1, 7 sc in same sp on Motif, 7 sc in next sp on Motif, ch 1, sl st in center ch-5 loop of same scallop on Center, ch 1, 7 sc in same sp on Motif and complete rnd as for 4th rnd of Center (no more joinings). Join and break off.

SECOND MOTIF . . . With Yellow work as for First Motif until 3rd rnd is completed. **4th rnd:** Attach White at tip of any cluster, 7 sc in next sp, ch 1, sl st in ch-3 loop of first free point following joining on First Motif, ch 1, 7 sc in same sp on Second Motif, 7 sc in next sp on Second Motif, ch 1, sl st in same center loop of scallop on Center as last joining of First Motif was made, ch 1 and complete as for First Motif, joining next 3 points of Second Motif to Center as First Motif was joined.

Make 10 more motifs, joining each to previous motif and to Center as Second Motif was joined.

EDGING . . . **1st rnd:** Attach White to first free point on any motif, sc in same place, * (ch 13, sc in next point) 5 times; ch 5, sc in next free point. Repeat from * around. Join. **2nd rnd:** * (In next sp make 8 sc, ch 3 and 8 sc) 5 times; 4 sc in next sp. Repeat from * around. Join and break off.

FLOWER CENTER (Make 13) . . . Starting at center with Black, ch 2. **1st rnd:** 5 sc in 2nd ch from hook. **2nd rnd:** 2 sc in each sc around. **3rd rnd:** * 2 sc in next sc, sc in next sc. Repeat from * around (15 sc). **4th rnd:** * Work off 2 sc as 1 sc, sc in next sc. Repeat from * around. Break off. Sew one to center of each flower. Starch lightly and press.

White Daisy Doily

MATERIALS: J. & P. Coats or Clark's O.N.T. Best Six Cord Mercerized Crochet, *Size 30, 1 ball (Small Ball) of Yellow, Size 100, 1 ball of White* . . . J. & P. Coats or Clark's O.N.T. Pearl Cotton, *Size 5, 1 ball each of White and Dark Orange* . . . Clark's O.N.T. "Brilliant," *1 ball of Hunter's Green. ½ yard of yellow organdy* . . . Steel Crochet Hooks No. 10 and No. 14.

CROCHETED BORDER . . . Starting at one corner with Yellow and No. 10 hook, ch 27. **1st row:** Tr in 11th ch from hook, (ch 3, skip 3 ch, tr in next ch) 4 times. Ch 7, turn. **2nd to 5th rows incl:** Skip first tr, tr in next tr, (ch 3, tr in next tr) 3 times; ch 3, skip 3 ch, tr in next ch. (One scallop completed). Ch 7, turn. **6th row:** Skip first tr, tr in next tr, (ch 3, tr in next tr) twice. Ch 7, turn. **7th, 8th and 9th rows:** Skip first tr, tr in next tr, ch 3, tr in next tr, ch 3, skip 3 ch, tr in next ch. Ch 7, turn. **10th row:** Repeat 9th row making ch 14 (instead of ch-7) to turn. **11th row:** (This starts second scallop.) Tr in 11th ch from hook, (ch 3, tr in next tr) 3 times; ch 3, skip 3 ch, tr in next ch. Ch 7, turn. Repeat 2nd to 11th rows incl, until 7 scallops (sections of 5 sps) have been completed. Break off. This completes one long side.

Attach thread to corner of first sp on last row and, working along side of this section, make ch 7, skip first sp, tr in next st, (ch 3, skip next sp, tr in next st) twice. Ch 7, turn. Continue making scallops as before until there are 5 sections of 5 sps, including the corner section, which was the last section of the long side. Work other sides

(Continued on page 38.)

Wild Rose Doily

MATERIALS: J. & P. COATS OR CLARK'S O.N.T. BEST SIX CORD MERCERIZED CROCHET, *Size 30:* **Small Ball:** J. & P. COATS—*3 balls of White and 2 balls each of Shaded Pinks and Shaded Greens, or* CLARK'S O.N.T.—*5 balls of White and 3 balls each of Shaded Pinks and Shaded Greens . . . Steel Crochet Hook No. 10.*

Doily measures 13 inches in diameter

LARGE FLOWER . . . With White, ch 20. **1st row:** Sc in 2nd ch from hook, sc in each ch across, 3 sc in end ch, sc in each ch along other side of starting chain. Ch 1, turn. Hereafter pick up back loop only of each sc.

2nd row: Sc in each sc to within 3 sc at tip, 2 sc in each of 3 tip sts, sc in each sc to end of row. Ch 4, turn. **3rd row:** Skip the sc at base of ch and next 3 sc, sc in next sc, (ch 4, skip 3 sc, sc in next sc) 3 times; (ch 4, skip 2 sc, sc in next sc) 3 times; (ch 4, skip 3 sc, sc in next sc) 4 times. Break off. This completes one petal. Work first 2 rows of a 2nd petal as for first petal, ending with ch 2, turn. **3rd row:** Sl st in end loop of first petal, ch 2, skip 3 sc on 2nd petal, sc in next sc, ch 2, sl st in corresponding loop of first petal, ch 2, skip 3 sc, sc in next sc, ch 4 and complete this petal same as first petal (no more joinings). Make 10 more petals, joining 2 loops of adjacent petals as

before (join last 2 loops of last petal to first 2 loops of first petal). Break off.

Attach thread to base of any petal and, working toward center, make 2 sc-rnds, 1 dc-rnd and 1 sc-rnd, decreasing as necessary to keep work flat by working off 2 sts as one.

ROSETTE . . . With Pink, ch 10, join. **1st rnd:** * In ring make sc, half dc, 5 dc, half dc and sc. Repeat from * 4 more times (5 petals). **2nd rnd:** * Ch 6, then, inserting hook from behind petals, work sc in ring between next 2 sc. Repeat from * around (5 loops). **3rd rnd:** In each loop make sc, half dc, dc, 8 tr, dc, half dc and sc. Sl st in first sc made. Break off. Sew this rosette to center of Flower.

LEAF . . . Starting at tip with Green, ch 15. **1st row:** Sc in 2nd ch from hook, sc in each ch to within last ch, 3 sc in last ch; sc in each ch along opposite side of starting chain, sc in same place as last sc. Mark last sc for base of leaf. Hereafter pick up only the back loop of each sc. Do not turn but work sc in each sc to within 3 sc from center sc at tip of leaf. Ch 1, turn. **2nd row:** Sc in each sc to marked sc, 3 sc in marked sc, sc in each sc on other side to within 3 sc from center sc at tip of leaf. Ch 1, turn. **3rd and 4th rows:** Sc in each sc to within center sc of 3-sc group, 3 sc in next sc, sc in each sc on other side to within last 3 sts. Ch 1, turn. **5th row:** Same as 3rd row but making sc, ch 7 and sc in center sc of sc-group at base of leaf. **6th row:** Sc in each sc to within ch-7 loop; 2 sc in loop, then pick up Flower and join leaf between 2 petals as follows: Ch 2, sl st in first loop to left of loop at tip of a petal, ch 2, 3 sc in ch-7 loop, ch 5, 3 sc in same loop, ch 2, sl st in corresponding loop of next petal, ch 2, 2 sc in ch-7 loop, sc in back loop of each sc across to within last 3 sts. Break off. Make 11 more leaves, joining each leaf between 2 petals of Flower as first leaf was joined.

Attach White to loop at tip of a petal, * ch 7, sc in first corner st of adjacent leaf, (ch 7, sc in next corner st of same leaf) twice; ch 7, at tip of leaf make sc, ch 7 and sc; (ch 7, sc in next corner st of leaf) 3 times; ch 7, sc in loop at tip of next petal. Repeat *(Continued on page 38.)*

Wild Rose
(Continued from page 37.)

from * around. Join and break off.

With Pink work a rosette as for center. Break off. Attach White to 5th st on any petal of a rosette, sc in same place, ch 7, skip 3 sts, sc in next st, then pick up doily and join rosette between 2 leaves as follows: Ch 3, tr in loop at tip of leaf, ch 3, sc in 5th st of next petal of rosette, ch 3, skip next loop on leaf, sl st in next loop, ch 3, skip 3 sts on rosette, sc in next st, ch 3, then, holding back on hook the last loop of each tr make tr in next loop on leaf and in corresponding loop on next leaf, thread over and draw through all loops on hook; ch 3, sc in 5th st of next petal, ch 3, sl st in next loop on leaf, ch 3, skip 3 sts on petal, sc in next st, ch 3, tr in loop at tip of leaf, ch 3, sc in 5th st of next petal, * ch 7, skip 3 sts, sc in next st, ch 7, sc in 5th st of next petal. Repeat from * once more. Join and break off. Make and join 11 more rosettes in this manner.

Now work a round of loops as follows: Attach White to tr-bar at right of loop which is at tip of leaf, ch 4, tr under next tr (at left of leaf), ** ch 3, sc in 3rd st from hook (picot made), ch 2, sc in next free loop on rosette, * ch 2, picot, ch 2, picot, ch 2, sc in next loop. Repeat from * 3 more times; ch 2, picot, then, holding back on hook the last loop of each tr make tr under next 2 tr, thread over and draw through all loops on hook. Repeat from ** around. Join last picot with sl st to 4th st of ch-4. Break off. With Green, work a leaf as before until the 5th row is completed. **6th row:** Sc in each sc to within ch-7 loop; 2 sc in loop, then pick up doily and join as follows: Ch 2, sl st in 2nd picot preceding joined tr's between rosettes, ch 2, 3 sc in ch-7 loop of leaf, ch 5, 3 sc in same loop, ch 2, sl st in 2nd picot after same joined tr's, ch 2, 2 sc in ch-7 loop and complete leaf as before. Make and join 11 more leaves in this manner. Make another leaf until the 5th row is completed. **6th row:** Sc in each sc to within ch-7 loop, in loop make 2 sc, ch 5 and 3 sc; ch 2, sl st in sc above center petal of rosette, ch 2, 3 sc in ch-7 loop, ch 5, 2 sc in same

loop, and complete leaf as before. Make and join 11 more leaves in this manner.

Now work 3 rnds of loops as follows: **1st rnd:** Attach White to tip of a leaf which is joined between rosettes, ch 7, sc in same place, * (ch 7, sc in next corner st) 3 times; tr in next free loop of rosette, tr in free loop of next leaf, (ch 7, sc in next corner st) 3 times; ch 7, in tip of leaf make sc, ch 7 and sc; (ch 7, sc in next corner st) 3 times; ch 7, tr in free loop of leaf, tr in next free loop of rosette, sc in next corner st of next leaf, (ch 7, sc in next corner st) twice; ch 7, in tip of leaf make sc, ch 7 and sc. Repeat from * around, ending with ch 7, sl st where thread was attached. **2nd rnd:** Sl st in next 3 ch, sc in loop, (ch 2, picot, ch 2, picot, ch 2, sc in next loop) twice; * ch 2, picot, holding back on hook the last loop of each tr make tr in each of next two ch-7 loops, thread over and draw through all loops on hook, picot, ch 2, sc in next ch-7 loop, (ch 2, picot, ch 2, picot, ch 2, sc in next loop) 6 times; ch 2, picot, then, holding back on hook the last loop of each tr, make tr in next two ch-7 loops, thread over and draw through all loops on hook; picot, ch 2, sc in next loop, (ch 2, picot, ch 2, picot, ch 2, sc in next loop) 4 times. Repeat from * around. Join last loop with sl st to first sc made. **3rd rnd:** Sl st to center of next loop, sc in loop, ch 2, picot, ch 2, picot and ch 2; sc in next loop, * ch 3, sc between picots of next free loop, (ch 2, picot, ch 2, picot and ch 2, sc in next loop) 5 times; ch 3, sc between picots of next free loop, (ch 2, picot, ch 2, picot, ch 2, sc in next loop) 3 times. Repeat from * around. Join and break off.

White Daisy
(Continued from page 36.)

to correspond, ending with a section of 3 sps. Sew last row to first section made to complete border. The scalloped edges are inner edges of border. Work sc closely along outer edges of border. Press border, place over organdy and sew in place with close blanket stitch.

DAISY (Make 6) . . . Starting at center with Size 100 White and No. 14 hook, ch 10. Join with sl st to form ring. **1st rnd:** 24 sc in ring. Sl st in first sc. **2nd rnd:** * Ch 14, sc in 2nd ch from hook and in each ch across, sc in next 2 sc on ring (one petal com-

pleted). Repeat from * around (12 petals). **3rd rnd:** * Working over 2 strands of White Pearl Cotton, sc in each ch of next petal, 5 sc in last ch; working over the 2 strands as before and over the sc's of petal make sc at base of each sc of petal, skip 1 sc on ring, sc in next sc. Repeat from * around. Sl st in first sc. Break off.

CENTER . . . Starting at center with Orange and No. 10 hook, ch 2. **1st rnd:** 5 sc in 2nd ch from hook. **2nd rnd:** 2 sc in back loop of each sc. **3rd rnd:** * Sc in back loop of next sc, 2 sc in back loop of next sc. Repeat from * around. **4th and 5th rnds:** Sc in back loop of each sc around. Sl st in next sc. Break off. Stuff center with cotton batting or scraps of thread and sew neatly in place.

LARGE LEAF (Make 2) . . . Starting at center with Green and No. 10 hook, ch 25 (the end of this chain is tip of leaf). **1st row:** Sc in 2nd ch from hook and in next 3 ch, ch 5, sc in 2nd ch from hook and in next 3 ch, sc in next 7 ch, sl st in next ch, turn, sc in next 5 sc, (ch 5, sc in 2nd ch from hook and in next 3 ch, sc in each sc and in next 5 ch, sl st in next ch, turn, sc in next 7 sc) twice; ch 5, sc in 2nd ch from hook and in next 3 ch, sl st in next sc. Break off. Working along opposite side of starting chain, attach thread to 5th ch from tip of leaf, ch 5, sc in 2nd ch from hook and in next 3 ch and continue to correspond with side just completed.

SMALL LEAF (Make 2) . . . Starting at center with Green and No. 10 hook, ch 12. **1st row:** Sc in 2nd ch from hook and in next 3 ch, ch 5, sc in 2nd ch from hook and in next 3 ch, sc in next 5 ch, sl st in next ch, sc in next 3 sc, ch 5, sc in 2nd ch from hook and in next 3 ch, sl st in next sc. Break off. Working along opposite side of starting chain, attach thread in 5th ch from tip, ch 5, sc in 2nd ch from hook and in next 3 ch and continue to correspond with side just completed.

Sew 3 daisies, a large leaf and a small leaf at each of 2 diagonally opposite corners as shown in illustration.

STEM . . . With Green make three chains of desired lengths for each flower group and sew in place as illustrated.

Illustrated on Front Cover

Daffodil Doily

MATERIALS: J. & P. Coats or Clark's O.N.T. Best Six Cord Mercerized Crochet, *Size 30:* **Small Ball:** J. & P. Coats—*2 balls of Bright Nile Green and 4 balls of Dark Yellow,* or Clark's O.N.T.—*3 balls of Bright Nile Green and 6 balls of Dark Yellow . . . Steel Crochet Hook No. 10 . . . Stamens.*

Doily measures 14 inches in diameter

Starting at center with Green, ch 12. Join with sl st to form ring. **1st rnd:** Ch 4, 32 tr in ring. Join with sl st to top of ch-4. **2nd rnd:** Ch 4, tr in same place as sl st, 2 tr in each tr around. Join. **3rd rnd:** Ch 4, tr in each tr around. Join. **4th rnd:** Ch 5, * tr in next tr, ch 1. Repeat from * around. Join to 4th ch of ch-5. **5th rnd:** Ch 6, * tr in next tr, ch 2. Repeat from * around. Join. **6th rnd:** Sl st in next sp, sc in same sp, * ch 5, sc in 3rd ch from hook (picot made), ch 8, sc in 3rd ch from hook (another picot made), ch 2, skip 2 sps, sc in next sp. Repeat from * around. Join. **7th rnd:** Sl st to center of next loop (between picots), ch 4, in same sp make 2 tr, ch 3 and 3 tr (shell made); * ch 3, in next loop between picots make 3 tr, ch 3 and 3 tr. Repeat from * around. Join. **8th rnd:** Sl st in next 2 tr and next sp, ch 4, in same sp make 2 tr, ch 3 and 3 tr (shell made over shell); * ch 3, shell in sp of next shell. Repeat from * around. Join. **9th rnd:** * Shell over shell, ch 4. Repeat from * around. Join. **10th, 11th and 12th rnds:** Shell over each shell, having 1 ch more between shells on each rnd. Join. Break off at end of 12th rnd.

DAFFODIL (Make 11) . . . Starting at base of Daffodil, with Yellow, ch 5. Join with sl st to form ring. **1st rnd:** Ch 4, 11 tr in ring. Sl st in top of ch-4. **2nd rnd:** Ch 4, tr in same place as sl st, * tr in next 2 tr, 2 tr in next tr (1 tr increased). Repeat from * around. Join. **3rd rnd:** Sc in same place as sl st, sc in each tr around. **4th rnd:** Sc in each sc around. **5th to 15th rnds incl:** Sc in each sc around, increasing 2 sc evenly in each rnd, being careful that increases do not fall over each other. **16th rnd:** Ch 4, tr in each sc around. Join. **17th and 18th rnds:** Ch 4, tr in each tr around, increasing 3 tr evenly around. Join. **19th rnd:** Sc in same place as sl st, * ch 5, sc in next tr. Repeat from * around. Sl st in first sc. Break off.

PETAL (Make 6) . . . Starting at base of petals, ch 18. Join with sl st to form ring.

FIRST PETAL . . . 1st row: Ch 4, 4 tr in ring. Ch 4, turn. **2nd row:** Tr in first tr, tr in next 3 tr, 2 tr in top of turning chain. Ch 4, turn. **3rd and 4th rows:** Tr in first tr, tr in each tr across, 2 tr in top of turning chain. Ch 4, turn. **5th row:** Skip first tr, tr in each tr and in top of turning chain. Ch 4, turn. **6th row:** Skip first tr, holding back on hook the last loop of each tr make tr in next 2 tr, thread over and draw through all loops on hook (a joint tr made), tr in next 4 tr; holding back on hook the last loop of each tr make tr in next tr and tr in top of turning chain and complete joint tr as before. Ch 4, turn. **7th row:** Skip first tr, holding back on hook the last loop of each tr make tr in next tr and in each following tr, tr in top of turning chain, thread over and draw through all loops on hook. Break off.

SECOND PETAL . . . Attach thread to ring, ch 4, 4 tr in ring, ch 4, turn and complete as for First Petal. Make 4 more petals in this manner.

Attach thread at base of petal, 2 sc in sp, 3 sc in next sp, in next sp make 2 sc and 3 half dc; 5 dc in next sp, 7 dc in next sp, in next sp make 3 half dc and 2 sc, 4 dc in top sp. Work along side to correspond. Continue in this manner all around outer edges of all petals.

Insert flower through ring of petals and sew in place. Sew stamens in place. Apply sizing to stiffen flowers in order to preserve shape. Sew flowers around doily as follows: Tack tips of 2 petals of each flower to 2 shells on last shell rnd of doily and tack together the points of the side petals of adjacent flowers.

FORMAL GARDEN

Runner measures 13 x 39 inches

MATERIALS: J. & P. Coats or Clark's O.N.T. Best Six Cord Mercerized Crochet, *Size 30:* **Small Ball:** J. & P. Coats—*12 balls of White or Ecru, or 16 balls of any color, or* Clark's O.N.T.—*18 balls of White or Ecru, or 20 balls of any color . . . Steel Crochet Hook No. 10.*

Each block measures 13 inches square.

BLOCK . . . Starting at center, ch 12. Join with sl st to form ring. **1st rnd:** Ch 3, 31 dc in ring. Join. **2nd rnd:** Ch 5, * skip 1 dc, dc in next dc, ch 2. Repeat from * around. Join to 3rd ch of ch-5. **3rd rnd:** * Sl st in next sp, ch 5, 3 d tr in next dc, 2 d tr in next sp, ch 5, sl st in same sp. Repeat from * around. Join. **4th rnd:** Sl st in next 5 ch, ch 5, holding back on hook the last loop of each d tr make d tr in next 6 d tr and in next ch, thread over and draw through all loops on hook (cluster made); * ch 11, make an 8-d tr cluster over the next ch, the next 6 d tr and the following ch, ch 19, make cluster as before over next group of sts. Repeat from * around. Join.

Now work in filet pattern as follows: **1st rnd:** Sl st back into last ch made, ch 6, * skip next cluster, tr in next ch (sp made), (ch 2, skip 2 ch, tr in next ch) 3 times; ch 2, skip next cluster, tr in next ch, (ch 2, skip 2 ch, tr in next ch) 3 times; ch 5, tr in same ch as last tr, (ch 2, skip 2 ch, tr in next ch) 3 times; ch 2. Repeat from * around. Join to 4th ch of ch-6. **2nd rnd:** Ch 6, (tr in next tr, ch 2) 8 times (8 sps made over 8 sps); * skip 2 ch, in next ch make tr, ch 5 and tr (corner sp made); (ch 2, tr in next tr) 12 times; ch 2. Repeat from * around. Join. **3rd rnd:** Ch 6, make 2 sps, * 2 tr in next sp, tr in next tr (bl made over sp), make 5 sps, 1 bl, tr in next 3 ch, ch 5, tr in same ch as last tr, tr in next 2 ch, tr in next tr (corner), make 1 bl, 5 sps. Repeat from * around. Join. **4th rnd:** Ch 6, make 1 sp, * 1 bl, ch 2, skip 2 tr, tr in next tr (sp made over bl), make 1 bl, 3 sps, 1 bl, tr in next 6 tr (2 bls made over 2 bls), make 1 bl, 1 sp, 1 bl in corner sp as before, 3 bls, 3 sps. Repeat from * around. Join. **5th and 6th rnds:** Follow chart. **7th rnd:** Make

8 sps, * tr in each st to within center st of corner, 7 tr in next st (corner bl made), tr in next 3 sts, make 5 bls, 11 sps. Repeat from * around. Join. **8th to 12th rnds incl:** Follow chart to end. **13th rnd:** Sc in same place as sl st, make 2 sc in each sp and sc in each tr around, having 7 sc in each corner sp. Break off. **14th rnd:** Attach thread to corner sc, 2 sc in same place, * sc in next 9 sc, (sl st in next sc, ch 6, tr tr in next 5 sc, ch 6, sl st in next sc, sc in next 20 sc) 3 times; sl st in next sc, ch 6, tr tr in next 5 sc, ch 6, sl st in next sc, sc in next 9 sc, 3 sc in next sc. Repeat from * around. Join. **15th rnd:** * Ch 10, (tr tr in next tr tr, ch 7, skip 1 tr tr, in next tr tr make tr tr, ch 7 and tr tr; ch 7, skip 1 tr tr, tr tr in next tr tr, skip 9 sc, in next sc make **2 long tr**—6 times over hook—ch **9, 2 long tr** in next sc) 3 times; tr tr in next tr tr, ch 7, skip 1 tr tr, in next tr tr make tr tr, ch 9 and tr tr; ch 7, skip 1 tr tr, tr tr in next tr tr, ch 10, sc in center sc of next corner. Repeat from * around. Join. **16th rnd:** * 10 sc in next sp, (9 sc in each of

(Continued on page 41.)

FORMAL GARDEN

(Continued from page 40.)

next 3 sps, sc in next 2 long tr, 9 sc in next sp, sc in next 2 long tr) 3 times; 9 sc in each of next 3 sps, 10 sc in next sp. Repeat from * around. Join. **17th rnd:** * Sc in next 40 sc, (sl st in next sc, ch 6, tr tr in next 5 sc, ch 6, sl st in next sc, sc in next 33 sc) twice; sl st in next sc, ch 6, tr tr in next 5 sc, ch 6, sl st in next sc, sc in next 40 sc. Repeat from * around. Join and break off.

Now work in rows: **1st row:** Mark with a pin the center of each scallop, attach thread to center sc of first scallop, ch 10, (tr tr in next tr tr, ch 7, skip 1 tr tr, in next tr tr make tr tr, ch 7 and tr tr; ch 7, skip 1 tr tr, tr tr in next tr tr, 2 long tr in sc preceding pin mark on next scallop, ch 9, 2 long tr in next sc) twice; tr tr in next tr tr, ch 7, skip 1 tr tr, in next tr tr make tr tr, ch 7 and tr tr; ch 7, skip 1 tr tr, tr tr in next tr tr, ch 10, sl st in center of next scallop. Turn. **2nd row:** 10 sc in first sp, (9 sc in each of next 3 sps, sc in next 2 tr tr, 9 sc in next sp, sc in next 2 tr tr) twice; 9 sc in each of next 3 sps, 10 sc in next sp, sl st in next sc on same scallop. Turn. **3rd row:** Sc in next 40 sc, sl st in next sc, ch 6, tr tr in next 5 sc, ch 6, sl st in next sc, sc in next 33 sc, sl st in next sc, ch 6, tr tr in next 5 sc, ch 6, sl st in next sc, sc in each remaining sc across. Break off.

Mark centers of scallops as before. Attach thread to center sc of first scallop on row just completed and work in scallop pattern until 1 scallop remains. Break off.

Work other corners to correspond. Make 2 more blocks the same way. Sew sides of blocks together at corresponding parts.

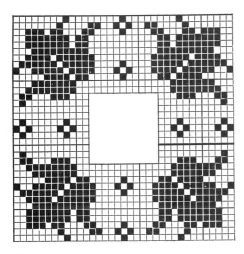

Chart for
FORMAL GARDEN

FLOWER FRAME

Runner measures 14½ x 40 inches

MATERIALS: J. & P. Coats or Clark's O.N.T. Best Six Cord Mercerized Crochet, *Size 30:* **Small Ball:** J. & P. Coats—*6 balls of White or Ecru, or 8 balls of any color, or* Clark's O.N.T.—*9 balls of White or Ecru, or 10 balls of any color . . . Steel Crochet Hook No. 10 . . . A piece of linen 10 x 36 inches.*

Each motif measures 2½ inches square.

FIRST MOTIF . . . Starting at center, ch 8. Join with sl st to form ring. **1st rnd:** Ch 7, (tr in ring, ch 3) 7 times; sl st to 4th ch of ch-7. **2nd rnd:** * Sl st in next sp, ch 4, 4 tr in same sp, ch 4, sl st in same sp. Repeat from * around. **3rd rnd:** Sl st in next 4 ch, ch 4, skip next 4 tr, tr in top of next ch-4, * ch 10, holding back on hook the last loop of each tr make tr in top of next ch-4, skip next 4 tr, tr in top of next ch-4, thread over and draw through all loops on hook (a joint tr made). Repeat from * around, ending with ch 10, sl st in top of ch-4 first made. **4th rnd:** * 13 sc in next sp, ch 1, 6 sc in next sp, ch 8, turn, d tr in ch-1 sp, ch 8, skip 6 sc, sl st in next sc, turn, 5 sc in next sp, ch 4, sc in 4th ch from hook (picot made), 5 sc in same sp, ch 6, in next sp make 5 sc, picot and 5 sc; 7 sc in next incomplete sp, ch 1. Repeat from * around. Join and break off.

SECOND MOTIF . . . Work as for First Motif until 3 rnds are completed.

4th rnd: * 13 sc in next sp, ch 1, 6 sc in next sp, ch 8, turn, d tr in next ch-1 sp, ch 8, skip 6 sc, sl st in next sc, turn, in next sp make 5 sc, picot and 5 sc; ch 4, sl st in corresponding loop on First Motif, ch 2, 5 sc in next sp on Second Motif, ch 2, sl st in corresponding picot on First Motif, ch 2, sc in 2nd ch preceding joining, 5 sc in same sp as last 5 sc were made, 7 sc in incomplete sp, turn work and make d tr in next ch-1 sp on First Motif. Repeat from * until next picot is joined to corresponding picot on First Motif, 5 sc in same sp on Second Motif as last 5 sc were made, ch 2, sl st in corresponding loop on First Motif, ch 4, in next sp make 5 sc, picot and 5 sc and complete rnd as for First Motif (no more joinings).

Make 12 motifs for each long side and 2 motifs for each short side, joining adjacent sides as Second Motif was joined to First Motif. Make 16 more motifs, joining 4 motifs (2 rows of 2 motifs) for each of 4 corners and joining these corners to sides.

Place crocheted piece over linen and cut linen 1¼ inches larger all around than inner edge of crocheted piece. Make ¼ inch hem around linen. Pin motifs in place. Make sc evenly around outer edges of linen, joining picots and loops with sl st to linen edge and making tr in each ch-1 sp at center of side of each motif.

Starch lightly and press.

Forget-Me-Not Doily

MATERIALS: J. & P. Coats or Clark's O.N.T. Best Six Cord Mercerized Crochet, *Size 30, 3 balls (Small Balls) of White* . . . J. & P. Coats Tatting-Crochet, *Size 70, 1 ball of Blue* . . . J. & P. Coats or Clark's O.N.T. Pearl Cotton, *Size 5, 1 ball of Orange* . . . Steel Crochet Hooks No. 10 and No. 14.

Doily measures 11 x 16 inches

Starting at one side, with White and No. 10 hook make a chain 17 inches long (15 ch sts to 1 inch). **1st row:** Holding back on hook the last loop of each tr make 2 tr in 5th ch from hook, thread over and draw through all loops on hook (cluster made), skip 8 ch, sc in next ch, * (ch 5 and complete a cluster as before in 5th ch from hook) twice; skip 5 ch, sc in next ch. Repeat from * across until row measures 15½ inches, ending with an sc. Cut off remaining chain. Ch 11, turn. **2nd row:** Make a 2-tr cluster in 5th ch from hook, sc between first 2 clusters, * (ch 5 and complete a cluster in 5th ch from hook) twice; skip 2 clusters, sc between the 2nd cluster skipped and the following cluster. Repeat from * across, ending with 2 clusters, skip last 2 clusters, sc in next st. Ch 11, turn. Repeat 2nd row until piece measures 10½ inches. Ch 8 to turn at end of last row. **Next row:** Sc between first 2 clusters, * ch 5, skip 2 clusters, sc between the 2nd cluster skipped and the following cluster. Repeat from * across, ending with ch 5, skip last 2 clusters, sc in next ch. Now work 2 rnds of sc closely around outer edges, making sc's as necessary at corners to keep work flat and joining each rnd. **3rd rnd:** * Sc in next 5 sc, ch 5, sc in 5th ch from hook (picot made). Repeat from * around. Join and break off.

FORGET-ME-NOT (Make 100) . . .
Starting at center with Blue and No. 14 hook, ch 5, 2 tr in 5th ch from hook, ch 4, sc in same place, (ch 4, 2 tr in same place, ch 4, sc in same place) 3 times. Break off.

Tack Forget-me-nots in place on doily at joinings of clusters as in illustration, making a French knot with Orange Pearl Cotton through center of each flower. Starch lightly and press.

NIGHT TABLE DOILY

ROYAL SOCIETY SIX CORD CORDICHET, Size 30:

SMALL BALL: 4 balls of White or Ecru, or LARGE BALL: 2 balls of White or Ecru.

Steel Crochet Hook No. 10.

Doily measures 14 inches square.

GAUGE: Each medallion measures 4¾ inches square.

MEDALLION . . . Starting at center, ch 8. Join. **1st rnd:** 12 sc in ring. **2nd rnd:** (Sc in next 2 sc, 2 sc in next sc) 4 times. **3rd rnd:** (Sc in next sc, 2 sc in next sc) 8 times. **4th rnd:** (Sc in next 2 sc, 2 sc in next sc) 8 times. **5th rnd:** (Ch 15, skip 7 sc, sc in next sc) 4 times. **6th rnd:** Sc in each ch around (60 sc). **7th rnd:** * Sl st in next 5 sc, (ch 9, remove hook and make a sl st on right side of chain 6 sts from end, ch 2, 3 dc in ring, ch 3, 4 dc in ring, ch 3, 3 dc in ring, ch 2, sl st in last sl st, ch 2, sl st in last sl st on sc-rnd—a flower made, sl st in next 5 sc) twice. Repeat from * around. Break off. **8th rnd:** Attach thread in 2nd dc of 4-dc group of 1st flower, sc in 2 center dc, * ch 19 (corner), sc in 2 center dc of 4-dc group of next flower, ch 10, sc in 2 dc of 4-dc group of next flower. Repeat from * around. Sl st in 1st sc. **9th rnd:** Ch 1, sc in each sc and each ch around, making 3 sc in 10th st of each ch-19 for each corner. Sl st in 1st sc. **10th rnd:** Ch 3, dc in each sc around, making 5 dc in center sc of 3-sc group at each corner. Sl st in top st of ch-3. **11th rnd:** Ch 1, sc in each dc around, making 3 sc in center dc of each 5-dc group at each corner (164 sc). Break off. **12th rnd:** Attach thread to 20th sc to right of any corner. * Make a flower, sl st in next 10 sc, make a flower, sl st in each sc to center sc of next 3-sc group, make a flower, sl st in next 10 sc, make a flower, sl st in next 10 sc. Repeat from * around. Break off. **13th rnd:** Attach thread in 2nd dc of 4-dc group of any corner flower, * sc in next 2 dc, ch 14, sc in 2 center dc of 4-dc group on next flower, (ch 9, sc in 2 center dc of 4-dc group on next flower) twice; ch 14. Repeat from * around. Sl st in 1st sc. **14th rnd:** Ch 1, sc in each ch and each sc around, making 2 sc in the 2 sc at each corner. Sl st in 1st sc. **15th rnd:** Ch 3, dc in each sc around, making 3 dc in each 2-sc group. Sl st in top st of ch-3. Break off. Sew 3 x 3 Medallions together.

EDGING . . . Sc in each sc around, making 2 dc in the 2 sc on either side of each joining, and 2 sc in the 2 center sts of each corner. Break off.

ROSE WHIRL

An enchanting bit of fine Irish crochet that will evoke admiration. A piece for your favorite small table.

MATERIALS: For best results use—

CLARK'S O.N.T. OR J. & P. COATS
BEST SIX CORD MERCERIZED CROCHET, Size 60:

SMALL BALL:

CLARK'S O.N.T. OR J. & P. COATS—*1 ball of White or Ecru.*

MILWARD'S *steel crochet hook No. 13.*

Completed doily measures about 9 inches in diameter.
Starting at center, ch 9, join with sl st. **1st rnd:** 16 s c in ring, sl st in 1st s c made. **2nd rnd:** S c in same place as sl st, * ch 5, skip 1 s c, s c in next s c. Repeat from * around, ending with ch 5. **3rd rnd:** * S c in next s c, 2 s c in ch-5 sp, ch 4. Repeat from * around. **4th to 15th rnds incl:** * Skip 1st s c, s c in each remaining s c of s c-group, 2 s c in ch-4 sp, ch 4. Repeat from * around (15 s c in each s c-group on last rnd). **16th rnd:** Ch 4, * skip 1 s c, s c in next 13 s c, ch 4, s c in ch-4 sp, ch 4. Repeat from * around. **17th rnd:** Ch 5, * skip 1 s c, s c in next 11 s c; (ch 5, s c in next loop) twice; ch 5. Repeat from * around. Continue in this manner, having 2 s c less in each s c-group and 1 loop more between s c-groups on each rnd, until 1 s c remains in each s c-group, and ending with ch 5, s c in loop preceding 1st s c. Now work as follows:

1st rnd: * Ch 2, s c in next loop; (ch 5, s c in next loop) 7 times. Repeat from * around, ending with s c

in loop preceding 1st ch-2. **2nd rnd:** * Ch 5, skip ch-2 loop, s c in next loop; (ch 5, s c in next loop) 6 times. Repeat from * around. **3rd rnd:** * Ch 5, s c in next loop. Repeat from * around. **4th rnd:** * Ch 5, 6 d c in next loop; (ch 5, s c in next loop) 5 times. Repeat from * around, ending with s c in loop preceding 1st d c-group. **5th rnd:** * Ch 5, s c between 3rd and 4th d c of d c-group; (ch 5, s c in next loop) 6 times. Repeat from * around. **6th rnd:** * Ch 7, s c in next loop. Repeat from * around. Fasten off.

FIRST ROSETTE... Ch 10, join. **1st rnd:** 24 s c in ring; join. **2nd rnd:** * Ch 5, skip 3 s c, s c in next s c. Repeat from * around (6 loops). **3rd rnd:** In each loop around make s c, half d c, 3 d c, half d c and s c; join. **4th rnd:** * Ch 5, s c in back loop of s c between this and next petal. Repeat from * around (6 loops). **5th rnd:** In each loop around make s c, ch 2, 7 d c, ch 2 and s c; join. **6th rnd:** Sl st in each of next 2 ch, s c in same place as last sl st, * ch 5, skip 3 d c, s c in next d c, ch 5, s c in 1st ch of next ch-2, ch 5, s c in 2nd ch of next ch-2. Repeat from * around; join to 1st s c. **7th rnd:** Sl st to center of 1st loop, s c in same loop, * ch 6, s c in next loop. Repeat from * around; join. **8th rnd:** Sl st to center of 1st loop, s c in same loop. Ch 8, s c in 5th ch from hook (p), ch 3, s c in next loop (1 p-loop made). * Ch 5, s c in center of 1 loop on last rnd of center piece, ch 2, s c in 2nd ch of ch-5, ch 3, s c in next loop on rosette. Repeat from

(Continued on page 47.)

44

SUNSHINE AND SHADOWS

A lovely effect—like sunshine playing on shadowy leaves—
makes the pattern of this unusual runner. Modern in feeling.

MATERIALS: For best results use—

CLARK'S O.N.T. OR J. & P. COATS

BEST SIX CORD MERCERIZED CROCHET, Size 50:

SMALL BALL:

CLARK'S O.N.T.—*10 balls of White or Ecru, or 18*
    OR   *balls of any color.*

J. & P. COATS—*7 balls of White or Ecru, or 10 balls*
          of any color.

BIG BALL:

CLARK'S O.N.T. OR J. & P. COATS—*4 balls of White*
                    or Ecru.

MILWARD'S *steel crochet hook No. 12.*

Completed runner measures about 18 x 42 inches.

GAUGE: 9 sps make 2 inches; 9 rows make 2 inches.

Start at right side of chart, make a chain 20 inches
long (18 ch sts to 1 inch). **1st row:** Tr in 5th ch from
hook and in next 19 ch (5 bls); * ch 3, skip 3 ch,
tr in next ch (1 sp); tr in next 8 ch (2 bls). Repeat
from * 23 more times; make 1 sp, 5 bls. Cut off remaining chain. Ch 4, turn. **2nd to 5th rows incl:**
5 bls over 5 bls below, * sp over sp, 2 bls over 2 bls.
Repeat from * 23 more times, sp over sp, 5 bls over
5 bls below. Ch 4, turn. Ch 7 to turn at end of 5th

(Continued on page 47.)

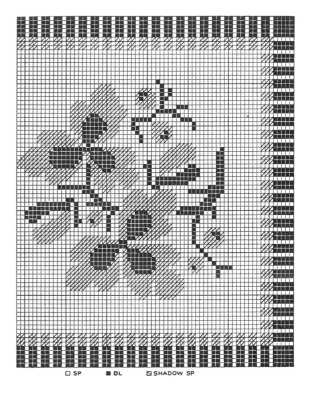

□ SP   ■ BL   ▨ SHADOW SP

CLOVER PATH

Runner measures 17 x 30 inches

MATERIALS: J. & P. Coats or Clark's O.N.T. Best Six Cord Mercerized Crochet, *Size 30:* **Small Ball:** J. & P. Coats—*9 balls of White or Ecru, or .12 balls of any color, or* Clark's O.N.T.—*12 balls of White or Ecru, or 14 balls of any color . . . Steel Crochet Hook No. 9.*

GAUGE: 4 sps make 1 inch.

Starting at narrow edge, ch 136 to measure 12 inches. **1st row:** Tr in 10th ch from hook, * ch 2, skip 2 ch, tr in next ch. Repeat from * across (43 sps). Ch 6, turn. **2nd row:** Skip first tr, tr in next tr, (2 tr in next sp, tr in next tr) 6 times (6 bls made over 6 sps); (ch 2, tr in next tr) 9 times (9 sps made over 9 sps); (make **1 bl**, 9 sps) twice; 6 bls, ch 2, skip 2 ch, tr in next ch (sp made over sp). Ch 6, turn. **3rd row:** Make 1 sp, tr in next 15 tr (5 bls made over 5 bls); (ch 10, skip 2 tr, tr in next tr, make

9 bls) 3 times; ch 10, skip 2 tr, tr in next tr, make 1 sp. Ch 6, turn. **4th row:** Make 1 sp, 4 bls, (ch 6, in next loop make sc, ch 2 and sc; ch 6, skip 3 tr, tr in next 22 tr) 3 times; ch 6, in next loop make sc, ch 2 and sc; ch 6, skip 3 tr, tr in next 13 tr, make 1 sp. Ch 6, turn. **5th row:** Make 1 sp, 3 bls, (ch 6, sc in next loop, ch 2, sc in next ch-2 loop, ch 2, sc in next loop, ch 6, skip 3 tr, tr in next 16 tr) 3 times; ch 6, sc in next loop, ch 2, sc in next ch-2 loop, ch 2, sc in next loop, ch 6, skip 3 tr, tr in next 10 tr, make 1 sp. Ch 6, turn. **6th row:** Make 1 sp, 2 bls, * ch 6, sc in next loop, (ch 2, sc in next ch-2 sp) twice; ch 2, sc in next loop, ch 6, skip 3 tr, sc in next 10 tr. Repeat from * 2 more times; ch 6, sc in next loop, (ch 2, sc in next ch-2 sp) twice; ch 2, sc in next loop, ch 6, skip 3 tr, tr in next 7 tr, make 1 sp. Ch 6, turn. **7th row:** Make 1 sp, 1 bl, * ch 8, sc in next loop, (ch 2, sc in next ch-2 sp) 3 times; ch 2, sc in next loop,

ch 8, skip 3 tr, tr in next 4 tr. Repeat from * across, ending with a sp. Ch 6, turn. **8th row:** Make 2 sps, * tr in next 3 ch (1 bl made over loop), ch 8, (sc in next sp, ch 2) 3 times; sc in next sp, ch 8, skip 5 ch, tr in next 3 ch, tr in next tr, ch 10, skip 2 tr, tr in next tr. Repeat from * 2 more times; tr in next 3 ch, ch 8, (sc in next sp, ch 2) 3 times; sc in next sp, ch 8, skip 5 ch, tr in next 3 ch, tr in next tr, make 2 sps. Ch 6, turn. **9th row:** 2 sps, 1 bl, * tr in next 3 ch, ch 8, (sc in next ch-2 sp, ch 2) twice; sc in next ch-2 sp, ch 8, skip 5 ch of next ch-8, tr in next 3 ch, tr in next tr, ch 6, in next loop make sc, ch 2 and sc; ch 6, skip 3 tr, tr in next tr. Repeat from * across, ending with tr in next 4 tr, 2 sps. Ch 6, turn. **10th row:** 2 sps, 2 bls, * tr in next 3 ch, ch 8, sc in next two ch-2 sps, ch 8, skip 5 ch of next ch-8, tr in next 3 ch, tr in next tr, ch 6, sc in next loop, (ch 2, sc in next loop) twice; ch 6,

(Continued on page 47.)

CLOVER PATH
(Continued from page 46.)

skip 3 tr, tr in next tr. Repeat from * across, ending with tr in next 7 tr, 2 sps. Ch 6, turn.

Starting with the 11th row on chart, follow chart to C. Follow chart from B to C until 76 rows are completed. Work end of Runner to correspond with beginning, following chart backward from D to A.

EDGING . . . 1st rnd: Ch 4 and, working along long side, make 5 tr in same sp and 3 tr in each sp around, making 11 tr in each corner sp, and ending rnd with 5 tr in first sp. Join. **2nd rnd:** Ch 6, 4 tr tr in same place as sl st, 3 tr tr in next tr, tr tr in next 7 tr, * ch 12, skip 11 tr, 3 tr tr in next tr, ch 12, skip 11 tr, tr tr in next 3 tr, 2 tr tr in next tr, tr tr in next 3 tr. Repeat from * across 6 more times, skipping 12 instead of 11 tr, ch 12, skip 11 tr, 3 tr tr in next tr, ch 12, skip 11 tr, tr tr in next 7 tr, 3 tr tr in next tr, 5 tr tr in next tr, 3 tr tr in next tr, tr tr in next 7 tr, ch 12, skip 11 tr, 3 tr tr in next tr and continue as on long side, skipping 12 tr instead of 11 tr under the 4 center ch-12 sps. Continue in this manner all around outer edges, working corners as before. Join. **3rd rnd:** Ch 9, ** (tr tr in next tr tr, ch 3) 4 times; (skip next tr tr, tr tr in next tr tr, ch 3) 5 times; * (5 sc in next sp, ch 3) twice; (tr tr in next tr tr, ch 3) 8 times. Repeat from * across, ending with 5 sc in last ch-12 sp preceding corner, (ch 3, skip 1 tr tr, tr tr in next tr tr) 6 times; ch 3. Repeat from ** around. Join. **4th rnd:**

Sl st in next sp, ch 5, holding back on hook the last loop of each d tr make 2 d tr in same sp, thread over and draw through all loops on hook (cluster made); (ch 7, make a 3-d tr cluster in next sp) 5 times; ** ch 7, skip next sp, (cluster in next sp, ch 7) twice; * skip next ch-3, sc in next ch-3 loop, (ch 7, skip next ch-3 sp, cluster in next sp) twice; (ch 7, cluster in next sp) twice; ch 7, skip next sp, cluster in next sp, ch 7. Repeat from * across, ending with sc in last ch-3 loop preceding corner, ch 7, skip next ch-3, (cluster in next sp, ch 7) twice; skip next sp,

cluster in next sp, (ch 7, cluster in next sp) 7 times. Repeat from ** around. Join to tip of first cluster. **5th rnd:** Sl st in next 3 ch, sc in same loop, (ch 10, sc in next loop) 6 times; * ch 13, skip next 2 loops, sc in next loop, (ch 10, sc in next loop) 3 times. Repeat from * across, ending with ch 13, sc in first loop between clusters at corner, (ch 10, sc in next loop) 10 times; ch 13, skip next 2 loops, sc in next loop, ch 10 and continue in this manner all around, working over corners as before. Join and break off.

Starch lightly and press.

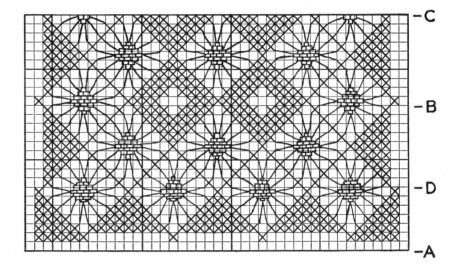

ROSE WHIRL
(Continued from page 44.)

*5 more times (6 loops joined). Make a p-loop in all remaining loops of rosette; join (12 free p-loops). Fasten off.

SECOND ROSETTE . . . Work 1st 7 rnds as for first rosette. **8th rnd:** Sl st to center of 1st loop, s c in same loop, make 1 p-loop; then join to 1st rosette as follows: Ch 5, s c in p of 2nd free loop after last joining on 1st rosette; (ch 2, s c in 2nd ch of ch-5, ch 3, s c in next loop on rosette, ch 5, s c in next p on 1st rosette) twice—*this 3rd joining is made in the p of the last joining of 1st rosette to center*—ch 2, s c in 2nd ch of ch-5, ch 3, s c in next loop on rosette. Join next 5 loops of 2nd rosette to next 5 loops on center in same way as 1st rosette was joined. Make a p-loop in all remaining loops of rosette; join (10 free p-loops).

Make 11 more rosettes, joining in same way and taking care to join the last rosette on both sides.

SUNSHINE and SHADOWS
(Continued from page 45.)

row. **6th row:** Skip 3 tr, tr in next tr (sp); ch 3, skip 3 tr, tr in next tr (another sp); 3 more sps, ch 1, skip 1 ch of next sp, tr in next ch, ch 1, tr in next tr (a shadow sp). Make 2 more shadow sps, * 1 sp, 2 shadow sps. Repeat from * 22 more times, make a shadow sp, 5 sps. Ch 4, turn. **7th row:** 3 tr in next sp, tr in next tr (bl over sp); 4 more bls over sps below; (ch 1, tr in next tr) twice—*a shadow sp over a shadow sp*. Make 2 more shadow sps, * a sp, 2 shadow sps. Repeat from * 21 more times; make 1 sp, 3 shadow sps, 5 bls. Ch 4, turn. **8th row:** Same as 7th row, but make ch-7 (instead of ch-4) to turn. **9th row:** 5 sps, * ch 3, skip 2 shadow sps, tr in next tr. Repeat from * across, ending with 5 sps over last 5 bls. Ch 4, turn. **10th and 11th rows:** Same as 7th and 8th rows. **12th to 15th rows incl:** Repeat 9th, 10th, 11th and 9th rows. **16th row:** 5 bls, 3 shadow sps, 15 sps, 1 bl, 51 sps, 3 shadow sps, 5 bls. Ch 4, turn and follow chart to end. Now repeat 9th, 10th and 11th rows 18 more times. Then repeat the 9th row once more. Now reverse chart and work back to the 1st row. Fasten off.

Simple Crochet Stitches

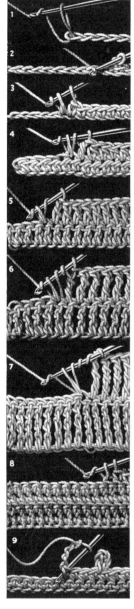

No. 1—Chain Stitch (CH) Form a loop on thread insert hook on loop and pull thread through tightening threads. Thread over hook and pull through last chain made. Continue chains for length desired.

No. 2—Slip Stitch (SL ST) Make a chain the desired length. Skip one chain, * insert hook in next chain, thread over hook and pull through stitch and loop on hook. Repeat from *. This stitch is used in joining and whenever an invisible stitch is required.

No. 3—Single Crochet (S C) Chain for desired length, skip 1 ch, * insert hook in next ch, thread over hook and pull through ch. There are now 2 loops on hook, thread over hook and pull through both loops, repeat from *. For succeeding rows of s c, ch 1, turn insert hook in top of next st taking up both threads and continue same as first row.

No. 4—Short Double Crochet (S D C) Ch for desired length thread over hook, insert hook in 3rd st from hook, draw thread through (3 loops on hook), thread over and draw through all three loops on hook. For succeeding rows, ch 2, turn.

No. 5—Double Crochet (D C) Ch for desired length, thread over hook, insert hook in 4th st from hook, draw thread through (3 loops on hook) thread over hook and pull through 2 loops thread over hook and pull through 2 loops. Succeeding rows, ch 3, turn and work next d c in 2nd d c of previous row. The ch 3 counts as 1 d c.

No. 6—Treble Crochet (TR C) Ch for desired length, thread over hook twice insert hook in 5th ch from hook draw thread through (4 loops on hook) thread over hook pull through 2 loops thread over, pull through 2 loops, thread over, pull through 2 loops. For succeeding rows ch 4, turn and work next tr c in 2nd tr c of previous row. The ch 4 counts as 1 tr c.

No. 7—Double Treble Crochet (D TR C) Ch for desired length thread over hook 3 times insert in 6th ch from hook (5 loops on hook) and work off 2 loops at a time same as tr c. For succeeding rows ch 5 turn and work next d tr c in 2nd d tr c of previous row. The ch 5 counts as 1 d tr c.

No. 8—Rib Stitch. Work this same as single crochet but insert hook in back loop of stitch only. This is sometimes called the slipper stitch.

No. 9—Picot (P) There are two methods of working the picot. (A) Work a single crochet in the foundation, ch 3 or 4 sts depending on the length of picot desired, sl st in top of s c made. (B) Work an s c, ch 3 or 4 for picot and s c in same space. Work as many single crochets between picots as desired.

No. 10—Open or Filet Mesh (O M.) When worked on a chain work the first d c in 8th ch from hook * ch 2, skip 2 sts, 1 d c in next st, repeat from *. Succeeding rows ch 5 to turn, d c in d c, ch 2, d c in next d c, repeat from *.

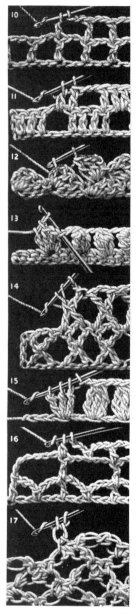

No. 11—Block or Solid Mesh (S M) Four double crochets form 1 solid mesh and 3 d c are required for each additional solid mesh. Open mesh and solid mesh are used in Filet Crochet.

No. 12—Slanting Shell St. Ch for desired length, work 2 d c in 4th st from hook, skip 3 sts, sl st in next st, * ch 3, 2 d c in same st with sl st, skip 3 sts, sl st in next st. Repeat from *. **2nd Row.** Ch 3, turn 2 d c in sl st, sl st in 3 ch loop of shell in previous row, * ch 3, 2 d c in same space, sl st in next shell, repeat from *.

No. 13—Bean or Pop Corn Stitch. Work 3 d c in same space, drop loop from hook insert hook in first d c made and draw loop through, ch 1 to tighten st.

No. 14—Cross Treble Crochet. Ch for desired length, thread over twice, insert in 5th st from hook, * work off two loops, thread over, skip 2 sts, insert in next st and work off all loops on needle 2 at a time, ch 2, d c in center to complete cross. Thread over twice, insert in next st and repeat from *.

No. 15—Cluster Stitch. Work 3 or 4 tr c in same st always retaining the last loop of each tr c on needle, thread over and pull through all loops on needle.

No. 16—Lacet St. Ch for desired length, work 1 s c in 10th st from hook, ch 3 skip 2 sts, 1 d c in next st, * ch 3, skip 2 sts, 1 s c in next st, ch 3, skip 2 sts 1 d c in next st, repeat from * to end of row, 2nd row, d c in d c, ch 5 d c in next d c.

No. 17—Knot Stitch (Sometimes Called Lovers Knot St.) Ch for desired length, * draw a ¼ inch loop on hook, thread over and pull through ch, s c in single loop of st, draw another ¼ inch loop, s c into loop, skip 4 sts, s c in next st, repeat from *. To turn make ⅜″ knots, * s c in loop at right of s c and s c in loop at left of s c of previous row, 2 knot sts and repeat from *.